"Change is inevitable, but it's how you manage it that defines your outcomes. Curt and Katie, with their extensive experience and deep understanding of the intricacies of disruption, deliver a tour de force that not only captures the essence of change management but also imparts practical wisdom. This book serves as a beacon, illuminating the path toward embracing disruption as an opportunity rather than a threat."

–MATT DERELLA, CEO of Catalyte and former Chief
Customer Officer of Twitter

"*The Responsive Enterprise* is a game changer. This book provides a powerful blueprint for transforming organizations to not just survive but thrive in an era of constant change. With its practical steps and inspiring real-life examples, it equips leaders with the tools to embrace change and turn it into a competitive advantage, setting their companies on a path to success."

–PETER BREGMAN, CEO of Bregman Partners and bestselling author
of *18 Minutes* and *Leading with Emotional Courage*

"As a triathlete and global executive, I believe that preparing our teams to adapt is the muscle memory we all need to build in our organizations. The principles and real-world stories outlined in this book can help you chart your own path to becoming an enterprise that embraces change and powers forward."

–RHONDA VETERE, Global Technology Executive
and STEM Ambassador

"Many companies want to be customer-centric, responsive, and agile but don't know how to methodically examine their internal processes, structures, and behaviors—the building blocks of their workplace culture—to truly understand what that looks like and what they might need to change to get there. This book will tell you exactly what you need to know!"

–MADDIE GRANT, Digital Strategist and Culture Designer at Propel

"Change initiatives are often platitudes on a plaque. But knowing the steps to effectively implement changes resulting in better business is quite different—it requires an ability to act with purpose and speed. Schwab and Markwell have created the guidebook to ensure the changes in your organization don't become buzzwords, but result in competitive differentiators."

–DR. NATALIE PETOUHOFF, *WSJ* bestselling author of *Empathy in Action*

The
Responsive
Enterprise

The Responsive Enterprise

TRANSFORM YOUR ORGANIZATION *to* THRIVE *on* CHANGE

Curt Schwab *and* Katie Markwell

IDEAPRESS
PUBLISHING

WASHINGTON, DC

IDEAPRESS
PUBLISHING

Printed in the United States

Ideapress Publishing | www.ideapresspublishing.com

All trademarks are the property of their respective companies.

Cover Design: James Iacobelli
Interior Design: Jessica Angerstein

Cataloging-in-Publication Data is on file with the Library of Congress.

Hardcover ISBN: 978-1-64687-136-0

Special Sales
Ideapress Books are available at a special discount for bulk purchases for sales promotions and premiums, or for use in corporate training programs. Special editions, including personalized covers, a custom foreword, corporate imprints, and bonus content, are also available.

1 2 3 4 5 6 7 8 9 10

CONTENTS

FOREWORD

The world of work has changed. In today's fast-paced business land-scape, we all navigate uncharted territory at speed, from hybrid work to generative AI to digital transformation. Change in all forms is the norm, simultaneously offering opportunity and challenge.

As leaders and decision-makers, we can no longer succeed solely by extracting more efficiency than the competition from our processes and teams. Instead, we must adapt to meet the growing demands of our customers and employees, who desire a more tailored, flexible, and pur-pose-driven approach in all touchpoints with our organizations.

To meet those needs, we must build change and innovation as ongo-ing expectations and critical skills for the future. According to the World Economic Forum's recently released 2023 Future of Jobs Report, cre-ativity, resiliency, flexibility, and agility are all skills expected to become more valued by 2027.[1] The businesses that are Randstad's customers also seek these qualities: the most adaptive companies consistently deliver better business results, from sales growth to share price.

These organizations are responsive enterprises. This book delves into the qualities, strategies, and mindsets necessary to build and nurture a responsive enterprise—a thriving organization capable of embracing and leveraging change to its advantage.

At the core of the responsive enterprise are people who lean into technology and three qualities. The first quality is a customer-centric mindset that permeates every facet of the organization. We must become relentless data gatherers, leveraging insights to drive informed decisions and deliver value to our customers and all stakeholders. We must strive to simplify the experience of our customers, employees, suppliers, and partners.

Operational excellence, the second quality, is a mandate to drive value creation—designing processes and building systems that balance efficiency with flexibility. Large organizations are complex, interconnected systems of people. Bringing people together with intentionality contributes to creativity, innovation, and higher output. Each person understands how he or she can uniquely provide value and support change.

The third quality, enterprise agility, becomes part of the organizational culture in the form of continuous actions and iterations at speed. Empowering teams to experiment and make rapid decisions to meet customers' ever-evolving needs becomes the norm. In this environment, diversity of thought is encouraged, and even perceived failures are opportunities for change and learning. Nurturing this culture of collaboration and belonging can unleash a workforce's full potential, enabling organizations to tap into innovation, even amidst continuous change.

Technology enables all these qualities. A company's ability to flex technology to identify, prioritize, and address business and market shifts is critical to the achievement of a digital strategy and, increasingly, an organizational one too. Artificial intelligence, the Internet of Things, and cloud computing continue to change our way of working and create a labor market that relies heavily on digital skills.

Throughout this book, you will find examples of teams who have embraced these qualities, such as the financial services institution that empowered cross-functional teams to identify and eliminate customer pain points, dramatically increasing satisfaction and significantly reducing service calls. You will learn from the massive health services company that transformed its scheduling systems to efficiently respond to the unprecedented challenges of COVID-19 and from the technology division that defied the constraints of its own growth, embracing agility to streamline decision-making.

We have also included four steps to becoming more responsive as a team and enterprise: 1) communication to align teams and actions to value, 2) systems thinking that provides a holistic perspective on change, 3) empowered teams that make informed decisions swiftly, and 4) feedback loops that enable rapid course corrections. These four repeating steps empower individuals at all levels of the organization to make decisions and act with purpose and speed when faced with a need for change.

People hold the power to ignite and the power to hinder change. As a leader, it is imperative to nurture change as a crucial skill in your organization while also fostering a sense of belonging, security, and equality. Only when the people who make up an organization embrace new ways of working, are equipped with new skills, and feel able to share their best selves will organizations genuinely embrace change and thrive.

The responsive enterprise starts right now, with you.

Sander van 't Noordende

Part 1

THE RESPONSIVE ENTERPRISE IMPERATIVE

Chapter 1

CONSTANT CHANGE DEMANDS A RESPONSIVE ENTERPRISE

All businesses now work in an environment of accelerating change, often from unexpected directions. The COVID-19 pandemic exposed which companies are built to thrive on change—but as changes go, this is just the beginning.

Perhaps you believe that the pandemic was a once-in-a-century event that executives, no matter how prescient, could never have anticipated.

But these days, existential threats and company-changing opportunities happen all the time—and the change is accelerating.

Consider for a moment what we've collectively experienced in the last few years leading up to the moment at which we're writing this, in mid-2023. Businesses have had to weather an unsettled political environment in the US, with two presidential impeachments and violence during the transfer of power to a new administration. The UK parted ways with the European Union in the schism known as Brexit; then Europe withstood a major war and streams of refugees as Russia attacked Ukraine. The global pandemic upended everything from health care and supply chains to the fundamental ways people collaborated in person and online. For the first time in decades, we experienced a stubborn surge of inflation and a series of major bank failures.

Waves of disruption are upending every industry. In finance, everything from loans to investing is now digital, and people pay for nearly everything digitally, with cards or tools like Venmo. Every major retail chain is now a hybrid of online or mobile shopping and bricks-and-mortar. Cars are becoming electric and autonomous, demanding huge investments from major automotive companies and changing the way we think about mobility. Entertainment is rapidly shifting from broadcast to on-demand streaming, transforming traditional distribution relationships and collapsing the once pivotal role of movie exhibition.

The World Economic Forum estimates that automation and artificial intelligence will disrupt some eighty-five million jobs by 2025.[2]

Global climate change looms on the near horizon, portending shifts in agriculture, real estate, transportation, travel, energy, health care, and geopolitics, and threatening the long era of stability that forms the foundation of the world we now occupy.

Change is now profound and pervasive. Becoming responsive is the only way for enterprises to survive and thrive.

Companies that thrive on change will dominate. But those companies are rare. Most established companies are built for a steady-state world where winning comes from extracting every last ounce of efficiency. That strategy is no longer sufficient and, sooner rather than later, will lead to decline.

This is a book about how to build a responsive enterprise that thrives on change. We'll tell you why that's important, how to think about it, how to implement it, and why technology is an element of all corporate responsiveness. That task may seem daunting, but with a systematic approach, transforming your company, department, or team to be responsive is not just possible, but imperative. A responsive enterprise is prepared for anything: not just to survive change, but to exploit it for competitive advantage.

For now, let's come back to the pandemic, which was likely the largest and most abrupt business disruption since World War II. Pandemic disruptions in where and how people worked upset long-established methods. Companies had to simultaneously deal with radical shifts in customer behavior, challenging conditions that prevented workers from collaborating in the usual places, and supply chain interruptions that interfered with long-established and efficient manufacturing processes.

But from a research perspective, the pandemic was revealing—it demonstrated how responsive companies were and how they dealt with upheaval and change. We worked with two companies that attempted to adapt themselves to the pandemic challenge. One thrived. The other stumbled. As you read these stories, ask yourself, what made the difference?

A MAJOR BANK FACING PANDEMIC CHALLENGES FINDS NEW WAYS TO SERVE CUSTOMERS

One of the largest banks in the US, with more than $300 billion in assets, tens of millions of customers, and tens of thousands of employees, was on a solid growth path when the pandemic hit. Like all banks, it faced huge challenges from the pandemic, including business customers managing government loans, retail customers who had lost their jobs, and branches that couldn't perform operations using the usual face-to-face methods.

Financial institutions have been transforming themselves for decades. To cite one notable market shift, banks that had established their competitive advantage through extensive ATM networks suddenly found that their customers wanted to deposit checks with mobile devices and pay each other with electronic transfers. The financial services companies best able to respond to changes like that were best positioned for coming changes.

The large bank we're describing—call it FinCo—had already spent years transforming its operations in three areas:

- It had focused on building a customer-centric strategy, creating competencies in areas like customer experience in applications and websites. As a result, even before the pandemic, it was making continuous improvements in the design of its branches, its website, and its emails to customers.
- It had built up its operational excellence using tools like process mapping, robotic process automation, and rigorous assessments of risks and controls to ensure that it could operate as efficiently and effectively as possible in any desired operation.
- It had focused on building enterprise agility at scale. For example, FinCo had more than 500 teams using Agile methodologies across twenty domains. The company moved these teams to a common system and process to ensure that the teams could connect their work to the company's priorities, and that executives could monitor and prioritize their progress based on corporate objectives.

As a result of this positioning, FinCo was poised to turn changes in its environment into competitive advantage. And that included the changes that COVID-19 was creating.

FinCo had been forced to close branches amid staffing shortages and reduced demand for in-person services. At the same time, its call centers were flooded with customers hoping to make transactions, asking about loans including the government's PPP (Paycheck Protection Program) loan regime, and resolving credit card issues. To respond to these needs, the bank rolled out customer-focused programs including delayed credit card payments and robust online banking features. But how would it make customers aware of these new services?

FinCo executives conceived a simple solution: a single rapid-response website that could act as a portal to all the answers a customer might want. The site needed to be accessible across any device and available to serve customers across all product lines in both English and Spanish.

The effort demanded collecting data across the organization in a broad and thorough discovery process. Because it brought leaders with divergent priorities together, the site project soon became central to the bank's customer-centric pandemic efforts.

Tapping the Agile frameworks and culture already in place across the organization, FinCo's Enterprise Digital Team worked with staff from across the organization to assemble accurate, helpful information to customers. The site went live within two weeks, an astoundingly short period of time for such a diverse task in such a large organization. And the team continually updated the site with new resources ranging from coronavirus-related identity theft, to travel disputes, to government relief efforts.

By April of 2020, 50,000 customers were visiting this robust online resource site daily to apply for credit cards, get car loans, make transactions, transfer money, obtain bank statements, and solve their immediate money issues. The bank updated the site 375 times within the first six months. Because of its focus on agility, the bank could process updates that previously took half a day in less than an hour.

Crucially, answers on the site were both up-to-date and searchable. This significantly reduced the load on the call center. FinCo's agility in standing up and updating the site were essential to enabling a quick and effective response to its customers in the midst of the pandemic.

MANAGING TECHNOLOGY IS CENTRAL TO SOLVING THE CHALLENGES COMPANIES FACE

It's impossible to disentangle the challenges companies face from changes in technology.

Technology enables new ways for anyone to interact with your company and influence your strategy. Well beyond e-commerce or mobile apps, now consumers expect to interact with their favorite brands on smart speakers like Amazon Alexa and smart wearables like the Apple Watch. They can interact in channels from Twitter to Instagram to Reddit. A dissatisfied consumer can go viral on YouTube or TikTok, submarining a brand without warning.

Meanwhile, within companies, the pace of slow-moving core technologies like databases and inventory systems is mismatched to the teams designing highly personalized and orchestrated interactions and customer journeys. Technology is at the center of every design process, and it seems like every product includes chips and internet connectivity. Marketing is now at least as much moderated by technologies like search engine optimization, email marketing, and targeted advertising as it is by ad copy and commercials. All those channels and products generate masses of data on who the target market is, what they want, and how their needs are changing on a month-to-month or moment-to-moment basis.

When there are failures, technology always seems to be somewhere in the blast radius. In 2023, Southwest Airlines saw years of investment in positive customer experience evaporate when its technologies for tracking the locations of planes and flight staff buckled under the load during a series of winter storms, stranding thousands of passengers.

The solution to building a more responsive enterprise centers on how you can enable solutions through technology, like FinCo's site for pandemic information, versus a focus on the technology itself. It's always easy to say "Why don't we just build x" to solve the problem, where x is the technology solution du jour. But it's never that simple. There are always ten or thirty or a hundred variations on x vying for attention. X is always connected in hard-to-manage ways to core systems of record like customer databases and product catalogs. There's always a need to fix the problems with x to match up to changing customer demands, market conditions, and competitive pressures.

In an environment like this, managing the speed and responsiveness of technology systems is central to the concept of a responsive enterprise. So the problem is not just the rate of change. It's the organization's ability to constantly flex technology to identify, prioritize, and address that change in ways that make a material difference.

IS CHANGE REALLY ACCELERATING?

You may be thinking: The pandemic was a once-in-a-lifetime black swan event, and things have always changed in business. And companies have always adapted. What's new now?

The pace is what matters. Change now happens more rapidly, more abruptly, and on a larger scale than ever before. To gather data on corporate responses to change, we commissioned Forrester Consulting to conduct a study on our behalf, contacting 418 North American digital strategy decision-makers.[3] About half agreed that business conditions are changing more rapidly than they were five years ago, in areas from competitive pressure to customer expectations—how companies communicate internally and externally (see figure 1-1).

These executives are right. Consider that it took twenty-eight years for credit cards to go from zero adoption to fifty million people, while it took twelve years for mobile phones to make the same leap. It took seven years for fifty million people to adopt the internet, but only three years for Facebook to pass that same milestone.

The smartphone era essentially began when Apple introduced the iPhone in 2007. By 2018, nearly everyone in developed countries had one. Companies in 2007 had to have an internet strategy. Within just a few years, their websites were completely obsolete, as mobile access and apps became widespread. Entire industries, including retail, travel, banking, and media, underwent complete transformations.

Change is accelerating even faster for companies with business customers. Procurement portals have replaced business-to-business sales reps in many companies. Software-enabled supply chains that were

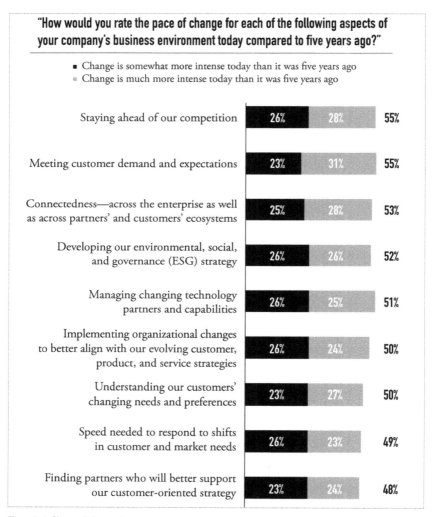

"How would you rate the pace of change for each of the following aspects of your company's business environment today compared to five years ago?"

- Change is somewhat more intense today than it was five years ago
- Change is much more intense today than it was five years ago

	Somewhat	Much	Total
Staying ahead of our competition	26%	28%	55%
Meeting customer demand and expectations	23%	31%	55%
Connectedness—across the enterprise as well as across partners' and customers' ecosystems	25%	28%	53%
Developing our environmental, social, and governance (ESG) strategy	26%	26%	52%
Managing changing technology partners and capabilities	26%	25%	51%
Implementing organizational changes to better align with our evolving customer, product, and service strategies	26%	24%	50%
Understanding our customers' changing needs and preferences	23%	27%	50%
Speed needed to respond to shifts in customer and market needs	26%	23%	49%
Finding partners who will better support our customer-oriented strategy	23%	24%	48%

Figure 1-1. Change is becoming more intense.
Source: A commissioned study conducted by Forrester Consulting on behalf of Celerity, November 2021. Base: 418 North American digital strategy decision-makers. Percentages may not sum to total shown due to rounding.

built on just-in-time delivery, minimal inventory, and global sourcing became rapidly obsolete after disruption from COVID and the Ukraine war; companies suffered an average of $182 million in losses per year.[4] The shortage in CPU chips alone crippled industries from cars to home security systems.

I (Curt) experienced the whiplash of change firsthand in my IT services firm, Blue Water. When I started the firm in 2001, companies knew very little about the internet and websites—the phone book was still the most common way to find a business. Companies only knew that they needed a website, and we rarely received pushback on five- and sometimes six-figure website design and development proposals for what we would now consider to be an online brochure. When it became clear that Google and other search results would ultimately replace offline business directories, we added search engine optimization to our suite of services. At first, clients asked us to build them a web presence. Shortly thereafter we met their needs with a digital marketing group that rapidly grew to be just as large as our web design and development team. Within a few years, the rage was e-commerce, which required us to master payment processing, online catalogs, and databases of product descriptions and photographs. This led to content management systems.

Then in the late 2000s, within less than a decade, people were expecting us to help them master social media tools like Myspace (remember that?), Facebook, Twitter, and Pinterest. As mobile swept in, it was like 2001 all over again. Everyone suddenly needed an app—even when, in most cases, an app wasn't an appropriate investment. While companies may need custom websites and mobile apps in some situations, the marketing services industry is now crowded with low-end commoditized agencies, automated web and app platforms, big-time platforms such as Sitecore and Adobe, open-source options, and interactive divisions of big advertising agencies. Even though we reinvented the company with each new market disruption, we still found ourselves in a tough environment for a midsize digital agency to survive.

Consider all the dominant companies swept aside, unable to deal with the pace of change. Blockbuster. Enron. Polaroid. Kodak. The Weinstein Company. Ringling Brothers. Borders. Sears. Toys "R" Us. RadioShack. Circuit City. Pier 1. A&P. In 2013, Microsoft bought Nokia's mobile phone division for $7.2 billion, then gave up on phones altogether within a few years. Philips, a huge consumer electronics company, exited the business completely and sold off its brand for just €150 million. Cisco, attempting to get in on the online video craze, paid $590 million for the trendy handheld video camera startup Flip Video in 2009, then completely shut it down just two years later.

What does all this mean for your company? Perhaps your entire industry will be challenged by an unanticipated market change like the ones that impacted Sears and Kodak, or challenged by a disruptive startup in the way that Netflix killed Blockbuster and now challenges traditional media companies.

Perhaps your competitors will merge and create a juggernaut that's daunting to compete with.

Perhaps you'll suffer as key workers and their knowledge walk out the door, wearied by the challenge of constantly rising pressures.

Perhaps some key shift in your customer base will accelerate, turning your business's nagging service, distribution, quality, or pricing problems into a rapid decline in market share.

Perhaps a startup will spend massively to build awareness in your market and put pressure on the traditional ways you do business.

Perhaps the question is not what the next change will be, since that's always hard to predict. The question is this: Is your enterprise prepared for change and able to respond quickly and decisively?

MANAGING VOLATILITY AND CHANGE ALL AT ONCE AND EVERYWHERE

Every company faced pandemic challenges in 2020 and 2021. A travel and hospitality company—call it TravelCo—was no different and faced massive disruption, not just from the dry spell in travel during the pandemic, but also from the rapid rebound in 2021. TravelCo had shed thousands of employees during the pandemic travel downturn and was challenged by uncertain, yet surging, demand on the other side. Post-pandemic travelers had higher expectations for features like contactless check-in but were willing to forgo other elements of their previous travel experience, like daily housekeeping.

All the change and uncertainty seemed to hit at once. The company was finding it increasingly difficult to respond to the demands of the new set of customers with fewer (and newer) employees. With shrinking capacity and unclear priorities, deciding which projects would get resources depended not on what would have the greatest impact on the business, but on which managers could marshal the greatest influence internally.

Adding complexity to the situation, multiple open positions and departures created institutional knowledge gaps around how to maintain and support architectures and applications that had expanded well beyond their original intent or use. Essentially, there was no systematic way to identify what customers needed, to prioritize projects that could satisfy those needs, and to complete those projects with a consistent way of working. Employee morale was shaken, and everyone felt like they were working multiple jobs.

We have worked with multiple organizations that faced these challenges or similar ones. Faced with too much change and with these problems unaddressed, leaders and organizations feel stuck and spend time treading water instead of swimming forward. If you find yourself stuck like this, we recommend five ways to move forward with the change mindset required of a responsive enterprise:

1. **Focus on prioritized outcomes.** Align the company on a single goal and prioritize projects based on alignment with that goal. Ruthlessly prioritize your customer in these goals and clear the decks for other work that does not move your goal forward.

2. **Establish a shared commitment to a way of working together.** Replace diverse and inconsistent collaboration models with a single interaction model built on trust, communication, and

embracing productive conflict. Embrace a discipline of structured meetings with consistent cadences, online collaboration tools, and respectful dialogue. Talk openly about commitment and agree how you will act when commitments or ways of working are broken (because they will be).

3. **Communicate again and again (and again).** For TravelCo, the team needed to once again unite around the idea of delighting and serving customers to rebuild morale. Keep the priorities, agreements, and changes you are driving forward front and center through frequent communications and dialogue teams.

4. **Develop a change network.** Change happens when people change their habits. Build up a team of change champions to encourage new habits and apply them throughout the organization.

5. **Celebrate and measure progress.** Find and communicate small wins throughout the process. And, remember, a "failure" is a win if you learn from it.

As TravelCo found, implementing these recommendations is challenging: You must identify customer priorities, a clear operational path forward, and an engaged team to make iterative improvements. But it's so much better than treading water or standing still in the face of change swirling around you. It's possible to create an enterprise that thrives on change—a responsive enterprise. There is a systematic way to do it. We will show you how.

THE THREE KEY DIMENSIONS TO BUILDING A RESPONSIVE ENTERPRISE

In the digital strategy decision-makers survey we mentioned earlier, no more than one in three showed signs of commitment to becoming more responsive. When asked to list their top three business goals, 41% included "Meeting customer demand and expectations" in the top three; 35% included "Understanding our customers' changing needs and preferences"; 35% included "Accelerating our response to shifts in customer and market needs"; and 36% included "Implementing organizational changes to better align with our evolving customer, product, and service strategies" (see figure 1-2). These numbers are encouraging but indicate only the will to become more responsive, not the ability. Only 36% of decision-makers say their companies consistently meet or exceed customers' needs and expectations.

Figure 1-2. Brands are increasingly customer-focused.
Source: A commissioned study conducted by Forrester Consulting on behalf of Celerity, November 2021. Base: 418 North American digital strategy decision-makers.

Based on our work with leaders at many dozens of companies, we have identified three crucial qualities that enterprises must embrace for maximum responsiveness:

1. **Customer centricity.** Orient business strategies to understand and deliver against customer needs.
2. **Operational excellence.** Align people and processes efficiently to deliver customer value.
3. **Enterprise agility.** Pivot existing business strategies based on market and customer insights to become more effective, adaptive, and resilient.

In traditional management consulting, improving these dimensions would be a matter of following professional best practices. But now that technology is entangled with nearly every action the company takes, things are more complicated. Any effort to improve customer centricity, operational excellence, and enterprise agility must address the role of enterprise technology in improving—or thwarting—efforts to be responsive.

Most companies are not improving on these three dimensions (see figure 1-3). We'll dive deep into all three of these in subsequent chapters. But, for now, let's examine each one a little more closely.

Customer Centricity

Our ability to identify
and respond to
customer needs

Operational Excellence

Our ability to adapt
to accommodate
changes in our
business environment

Enterprise Agility

Our ability to ensure
business continuity
through organizational
resiliency and adaptivity

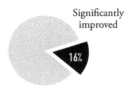

Significantly
improved

16%

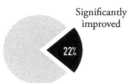

Significantly
improved

22%

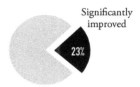

Significantly
improved

23%

Figure 1–3. Few companies are improving on key dimensions.
Source: A commissioned study conducted by Forrester Consulting on behalf of
Celerity, November 2021. Base: 418 North American digital strategy decision-makers.

Customer-centric enterprises are highly responsive to changes in customer needs

A customer-centric company must not only know what its customers want; it must also be able to act on those desires.

All major companies have research groups that are constantly probing customers' needs and desires. These groups use tools like post-purchase surveys, in-field observation, ethnographic research, and research from third-party survey organizations to identify shifts in customer needs. They augment this with knowledge bubbled up from frontline workers and sales and support teams.

Sometimes the changes become instantly and rapidly apparent. In the case of TravelCo, for example, executives soon learned of pandemic-threatened customers desiring to check into hotel rooms with as little human interaction as possible.

But the real challenge is with acting quickly on these shifts. This was Clayton Christensen's main thesis in his groundbreaking book *The Innovator's Dilemma*, which postulated that incumbent companies were often culturally and structurally unable to respond to disruptive competitive offerings that better met customers' needs.

Among decision-makers in our survey, 33% identified the lack of coordination across teams or organizations within the company as a barrier to responding to customer needs, and 32% cited the inability to manage and distribute relevant customer insights to the teams that needed them.

A customer-centric company has mechanisms in place to analyze shifts in customer journeys. It knows where problems are occurring and can test how to address those problems, using tools including customer research, journey mapping, analytics, and future mapping. We'll describe those techniques in more detail in chapter 3.

Most importantly, a customer-centric company must prioritize methods to address those shifts and mobilize its systems to implement those methods. It must find ways to move forward with changes that are not just desirable for consumers, but also feasible for the company and viable for improving its business goals. This includes organizing in ways that address customer experience improvements, measuring progress toward those improvements, and adopting new methods for engaging with customer needs, like design thinking.

Operational excellence aligns enterprises to deliver value

Customer centricity is not sufficient for responsiveness. Responsive companies must not only *know* what improvements are needed; they must also be able to act on those improvements.

Operational excellence reflects how well a company can move from vision and strategy to execution. It depends on mechanisms that align resources in the company to where the value is created. Operational excellence is a crucial element of responsiveness, because unless a company can mobilize its resources effectively, it has no way to be responsive.

Operational excellence rests on the three traditional pillars required to get anything done in a company: people, process, and technology.

On the people side, operational excellence needs leadership to craft a vision, develop a clear and concise road map, and communicate both effectively to employees. People doing the work need to understand the larger effort that they're a part of. This typically requires an organizational change management effort because that understanding is part of the company culture.

On the process side, operational effectiveness requires governance that allows people to identify problems and make improvements. Empowering teams to better serve customers is part of that effort. Rigid management structures get in the way; once people have the tools and understand the priorities in a responsive enterprise, they should be empowered to take the steps necessary to respond to market and customer changes.

Technology is central to operational effectiveness because workers throughout the enterprise use it every day and in every process. When that technology stays responsive to the needs of those professionals, the organization can move efficiently to address whatever challenges it needs. If those same workers are struggling with out-of-date technologies, they're unable to do what the organization needs quickly and effectively. Misaligned, unresponsive, poorly integrated, or out-of-date technologies destroy operational effectiveness.

As we describe in detail in chapter 4, improving operational effectiveness begins with foundational steps like analyzing the organization's operating model, continues with improving governance and measurement to align resources with value, and encompasses discipline in analyzing data from across the enterprise to sharpen the focus on what's working and what needs improvement. All of these efforts depend on understanding and improving the smooth functioning of the organization's core technologies.

Operationally excellent organizations have the people, tools, and technologies required to go from understanding customer needs to actually delivering on a strategy to fulfill them. But to apply those resources, they need a mindset of moving responsively. That takes agility.

Enterprise agility requires putting processes in place to be rapidly responsive

As a process to build software, Agile methodologies now pervade technology development. But as many organizations have discovered, there's a huge gap between *doing* Agile and *being* agile.[5] To be responsive, companies must cultivate a culture of enterprise agility.

Agility is a mindset and a movement. When led by culture and by mindset, the chances of a successful agile transformation increase powerfully, allowing a company to iterate, scale, and continuously focus on value and outcomes.

Enterprise agility starts from a foundation of company values. It demands defining big ideas for the company's employees to believe in, including a vision, a set of desired outcomes, and a road map for change.

With the vision in place, a company can begin to change, starting in the places within the company most hospitable to agile thinking. The change begins with small, integrated, and empowered cross-functional teams embracing Agile concepts and methods. Their success then spreads to other parts of the company.

In essence, enterprise agility takes the principles behind Agile software methodologies—including a product mindset, empowered cross-functional teams, and a high cadence of sprints to make improvements—and leverages them across large parts of the business. Agile methodologies can inform the governance and methods of any parts of the organization where continuous improvement makes a major difference.

Agile teams can act quickly and independently, secure in the knowledge that they're following a corporate vision. Agile principles include putting customer satisfaction at the top of the priority list, embracing the need and value for ongoing change, delivering new advances rapidly, and prioritizing action and experimentation over planning and output. Agile teams reduce risks by progressively iterating, measuring their progress against value and outcomes, and celebrating all successes, educational failures, and the elimination of waste. We describe these changes in more detail in chapter 5.

FinCo's progress on these values are what positioned it to succeed in the pandemic. The company had no way of knowing a huge disruption to its business was coming, but was nonetheless prepared to respond when the disruption arrived.

COMPANIES THAT RANK HIGHEST ON THESE QUALITIES HAVE BETTER BUSINESS PERFORMANCE

Few companies rank high on all three qualities of responsiveness: customer centricity, operational excellence, and enterprise agility. Based on our survey, we estimate that no more than one in six companies has a high degree of maturity on all three dimensions.

Those that do, however, demonstrate powerful advantages. They report six times better performance on their speed of response to changing customer and market needs, three times better on meeting customer demands and applications, and three times better on understanding customers' needs and preferences. These elite companies also show huge advantages on traditional measures like revenue growth, profit, earnings per share, market valuation, and share price. We'll explore these differences in more detail in chapter 11.

A company can get lucky once or twice based on market conditions. A company may discover and patent a fundamental innovation, take advantage of a competitor's stumbles, or catch the wave of a new technology trend. But the key is not whether a company can do this once. It is whether the company can turn response to change into an engine for constant growth and resilience. This is why responsive enterprises are more likely to be successful: When faced with challenges, they respond not just by surviving but by gaining advantage. When accelerating change is so pervasive, such companies will inevitably land on top.

THE DELIBERATE PATH TO BECOMING A RESPONSIVE ENTERPRISE

It is our goal in the rest of this book to give you all of what you need to embrace the principles of the responsive enterprise in your own organization. Here's what that includes.

In chapter 2, we explain how to get from here to there—how to initiate the transformation required to become a responsive enterprise. We describe four key transformation stages: exposing value, embracing systems thinking, empowering teams, and embedding feedback loops. We showcase this through the transformation that took place at a health care delivery company.

In chapter 3, we dive deeply into the discipline of customer experience. Customer experience is not just an arbitrary desire to make customers happy; instead, it is a set of methods for researching and acting on the customer journeys that lead to profit and loyalty. We'll show how a major financial company applied customer experience principles to grow and succeed.

In chapter 4, we examine the principles of operational excellence, including how to analyze a company's operating model and drive change to make it more efficient and responsive. We'll describe how this played out in a unit of one of the largest retailers in the world.

In chapter 5, we revisit the concept of enterprise agility. What does it take to evolve from the rigid structures of traditional management to the flexible and responsive systems required of an agile enterprise? We'll show how a large technology company embraced enterprise agility to reclaim a resurgent culture of growth.

In chapter 6, we discuss tracking value within companies: identifying it, exposing it, and aligning resources behind it.

In chapter 7, we explain how to embrace the discipline of systems thinking. All enterprises have complex, interconnected systems, and only a systematic approach can move the whole company forward together.

In chapter 8, we demonstrate the path to a key cultural value of responsive companies: empowering teams. The example in this chapter is a nonprofit, the Leukemia & Lymphoma Society.

In chapter 9, we reveal methods for embedding feedback loops and using them to fuel innovation. We'll show how the principles of feedback propelled success in adoption of a productive intranet at the health care provider OhioHealth.

In chapter 10, we tackle a paradox: If technology is so central to responsiveness, how can companies move forward quickly even when core technologies are rigid and beset by technical debt? We explore this in a case study about a financial services company faced with an unresponsive and obsolescing loan origination system.

Finally, in chapter 11, we'll examine what the future of responsive enterprises looks like and how responsiveness will define the landscape of competition.

The transformation to becoming a responsive company is not for the faint of heart. But the rewards are many. Those that embrace change and commit to being responsive enterprises will be the leaders for the next decade and beyond.

Chapter 2

THE RESPONSIVE ENTERPRISE TRANSFORMATION

This is the story of a chain of dialysis clinics—let's call it ClinicCo—that has a very big job to do: taking care of more than 300,000 patients with end-stage renal disease. Each of those patients needed to go to one of ClinicCo's 4,000 clinics at least three times a week for dialysis treatments.

That might sound like a health care problem. It's also a planning problem.

Inside each clinic are a limited number of dialysis chairs. Each chair can treat a single patient, typically for three hours per session. Nurses and other health professionals need to supervise the treatments. Each treatment needs purified water, chemicals, and equipment to function properly. Patients need to get checked in, treated, and checked out, with a sufficient interval between patients. And, of course, since ClinicCo needs to pay for all those employees and all that equipment, the patients and their insurance companies need to be billed properly.

What's essential to understand is that the set of tools and systems used to get all the staff and equipment in place and everyone doing their jobs is an operational necessity for ClinicCo. If the resource planning and execution happens properly, then the staff can serve the patients effectively, efficiently, and in compliance with all health and insurance regulations. The level of effectiveness of that system—and its ability to deal with and respond to both daily hiccups and longer-term shifts and trends in the health care world—defines success for ClinicCo on a daily basis.

In the end, the patients must be treated safely. The equipment must be used efficiently. The staff needs to go where they are most needed with neither dangerous understaffing nor wasteful overstaffing. ClinicCo needs to solve that multidimensional planning problem, not just once but every single day of the year, and the problem is never quite the same from one day to the next. It's like a high-stakes ballet where the choreography changes every day.

At a typical ClinicCo clinic, it was taking three full days to solve the scheduling problem for each three-day period—and that was assuming nobody took an unexpected sick day and no equipment broke down.

The scheduling challenge is a people problem and an equipment problem—but at its heart, it is a software problem. Any solution would involve software that the staff, as well as the doctors and patients, in the clinics would use. And any solution would touch all the other systems that ClinicCo used, including compliance, insurance, and payroll systems.

The first attempt to solve the problem was a homegrown software solution that we'll refer to here as "Scheduler," created by a product lead working with ClinicCo. Scheduler addressed ClinicCo's inefficient pen-and-paper scheduling in its United States dialysis clinics. But the number of possible solutions created a mind-boggling combinatorial multiplicity of options. How many options? Visualize a number starting with the digit 5 and continuing with 78 zeroes. That's a similar magnitude to the total number of atoms in the universe.

Partnering with ClinicCo, a specialized team at our organization built improvements and enhancements onto the Scheduler software, creating a tool that could optimize the schedule for more than thirty tactical, logistic, and patient-focused business rules that clinic scheduling staff had identified, all with the click of a button. We also created a report to score the potential schedules at each clinic on the desired variables.

These features took three months to roll out, and that was the beginning of a transformation at ClinicCo. Once deployed, the new Scheduler relieved staff of the need to move resources around by guesswork and intuition, vastly reducing the risk of over- or understaffing. Now that it took only 15 to 30 minutes to generate an optimized schedule—as opposed to up to three days—staff could repurpose that time on client care and efficiency. This time-saving improvement delivered millions of dollars in savings in both time and labor.

Solving a problem like this is never a one-off experience. An ordinary company implements the solution and hopes for the best. But a responsive company recognizes the potential to embrace the improvements and become continuously more responsive.

That's what happened at ClinicCo. The team at ClinicCo responsible for the Scheduler product looked for ways to expand the company's idea of what it could do with the scheduling system. For example:

- Manage a pool of staff that could be deployed across multiple local clinics, making best use of technically and medically qualified staff where they were most needed.
- Display critical patient data to more effectively track patients' needs and treatments.
- Develop an admission tool to onboard new patients.
- Integrate with Google Maps to help patients and staff get to the clinic most suitable for them.
- Create a portal for hospitals, making it easy for newly diagnosed renal disease patients to connect with an appropriate ClinicCo clinic.

Without the right practices in place, expanding software in all those directions could be a messy disaster—and could easily get out of touch with the staff's and patients' actual needs. But ClinicCo took three steps to make sure that the tool continued to evolve in the most effective direction.

First, ClinicCo promoted a better understanding of the patients' and clinic staff's needs by inviting our cross-functional team to visit the clinics. Software developers and other team members saw patients arrive on shuttle buses, watched them check in and get connected to the machines, and got a look at the huge purified water tanks and supplies of chemical reagents necessary for the dialysis process. They didn't stop with a single clinic either—they visited multiple locations and began to understand the diversity in clinic layouts and variations in methods that the software would need to address. This enabled them to create detailed and accurate assessments and diagrams of the activities within a clinic.

Second, ClinicCo recognized the interconnected nature of all the systems involved. An event like a snowstorm could affect patient schedules and clinic staff availability and ripple through multiple days. A change in the screen used to check in a patient might have an unexpected interaction with the screen used to connect to insurance information. Every potential modification had to be vetted for unexpected connections. The development team employed quality assurance staff skilled at identifying flaws and bugs that might result from the complex interconnections among systems.

And finally, the company embraced a product mindset and Agile development methods. This started with treating Scheduler as a customer-centric product where the users—the staff at ClinicCo—were the customers. There's no effective way to create a rigid road map for the development of a tool like the ever-expanding Scheduler. Instead, in true agile fashion, the road map was flexible and evolving, based on patterns of complaints and other issues that emerged as staff used the scheduling tool. The ability to quickly reprioritize tasks in the backlog of work facilitated an evolving road map, enabling the company to respond in days or weeks to the clinics' ever-changing demands and priorities.

All of these qualities came into play in 2020 when ClinicCo clinics began to deal with an unexpected and unplanned complication: COVID-19. The leaders within the company found they needed to be flexible in dealing with the problem. Some clinics had to be closed to Coronavirus-positive patients to safeguard the health of their other patients. Others created special seats or rooms specifically for those suffering from COVID-19, separate from those who had tested negative.

Suddenly, the company needed to rework Scheduler to accommodate the new reality—fast. Which fields needed to acknowledge COVID-19 status? How would COVID-positive or negative patients be identified, scheduled, checked in, and treated?

The Scheduler teams at both ClinicCo and our organization immediately got to work to update the software. Incredibly, within two weeks, the software team had created a new feature that included COVID status, and within a month, it was in use at all the ClinicCo clinics in the US.

How was this rapid response even possible? It required the three basic qualities of a responsive enterprise.

- Customer centricity: a clear understanding of how the clinics worked and what the patients and staff needed.
- Operational excellence: a focus on making the clinics as efficient and seamless as possible, across all the interlocking systems for tracking patients, staff, and treatments.
- Enterprise agility: a product mindset that promotes a readiness to flex based on new priorities, even with the emergence of a surprising development like the pandemic.

ClinicCo remains not just a health care delivery company, but one that uses ever-improving software and planning to efficiently deliver the best outcomes for patients. And its responsive nature is what enables it to continue to grow and remain adaptable, regardless of the complexity of the changing circumstances in which its clinics operate.

A FOUR-STAGE CYCLE FOR RESPONSIVE TRANSFORMATION

What started as a means to solve a scheduling problem eventually touched many parts of the organization's activities, from staffing and equipment allocation to check-ins, compliance, and referrals. ClinicCo's responsiveness as an organization grew and continued through changes in management and acquisitions of other dialysis companies, culminating in a company that could confidently look at a major systemic change like COVID and take rapid action.

ClinicCo didn't just adapt. It transformed itself into a more responsive company, one that embraced customer centricity, operational excellence, and enterprise agility in more and more of its ways of working.

This doesn't just happen on its own: It's part of a deliberate evolution toward responsiveness in all aspects of a company's strategy and operations over time. When companies undertake transformation efforts, success generally starts at the top, with a senior executive such as the CEO, president, COO, or chief customer officer taking responsibility. There must also be a set of processes and methods to initiate the change, communicate its value, and manage the adoption of the change throughout the organization. (We talk about this in detail in our discussion of organizational change management in chapter 5.)

Based on our research and real-world experience of how companies become more responsive, we've identified a four-stage cycle called "the four E's" that successful companies follow on an iterative basis, creating improvements in responsiveness in each iteration (see figure 2-1). The steps in the four E's are as follows:

1. **Expose the value of the transformation.** Determine how the transformation will create and enhance value in the organization, and then communicate that vision to those involved.

2. **Embrace an overarching philosophy of systems thinking.** Build the skill of identifying connections within the enterprise and between the enterprise and the outside world; intelligently analyze the effect on those connections each time a change is proposed.

3. **Empower teams to improve skills and make decisions.** As much as possible, push decision-making out to the teams in

closest touch with customers; encourage those teams to identify
and autonomously make constant improvements.

4. **Embed feedback loops in systems and act on data.** Build digital tools that generate data about the enterprise's people and
systems; leverage the data to make continuous improvements.

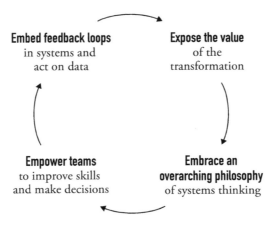

Figure 2–1. The four-stage cycle.

THE TRANSFORMATION MATRIX

You may be wondering how these four steps align with the three qualities
of a responsive enterprise: customer centricity, operational excellence,
and enterprise agility. The answer is that changes for any combination
of those three qualities go forward using the four stages: value, systems
thinking, empowered teams, and feedback loops.

We illustrate this with the transformation matrix (table 2-1), which
is fundamental to understanding the responsive enterprise transformation. You can use this matrix two ways. Read down the columns to

see how to build each of the three qualities. Or read across the rows to understand what subgoals you can pursue in each stage.

	Three qualities of a responsive enterprise		
Four-step process for responsive enterprise transformation	Customer Centricity	Operational Excellence	Enterprise Agility
Expose the value of the transformation	Identify where customer experience improvements can deliver value; promulgate a customer-centric mindset.	Align investment with value; broadly communicate the value of making changes; focus on outcomes, not just activity.	Clarify speed and direction; channel energy appropriately; remove antipatterns.
Embrace an overarching philosophy of systems thinking	Reveal how all staff and functions contribute to customer experience.	Create integrated plans, so all progress moves forward in step.	Get teams working in tandem to move the whole organization forward.
Empower teams to improve skills and make decisions	Build a culture of conscientious contributors acting autonomously; develop creativity, design, and innovation skills.	Develop skills in change management and value-based decision-making.	Develop skills in continuous learning; adopt a growth mindset.
Embed feedback loops in systems and act on data	Clearly identify customer success metrics; measure ongoing progress; identify opportunities for improvement.	Build a system to track and monitor progress; make results accessible to teams and customers.	Focus on short bursts of activity and constant feedback versus long tail milestones; test small experiments frequently.

Table 2–1. The transformation matrix.

Let's examine how each of the four steps moves an organization closer to becoming a more responsive enterprise, with examples from the transformation at ClinicCo. Each subsection below corresponds to reading across one row of the transformation matrix.

Expose the value of the transformation

Any transformational effort worth doing will make significant changes in the work of hundreds or thousands of people. A shift of that magnitude cannot happen without a clear understanding of the value of the proposed transformation to the enterprise.

The purpose of these transformations is to allow organizations to be more responsive. But speed alone is not sufficient. Direction is crucial as well, so the transformation can become a coordinated and worthwhile effort.

This starts with identifying the problem. For example, at ClinicCo, the problem was the scheduling challenges and that the scheduling software could not appropriately assign resources for maximum efficiency. Here's how the concept of exposing value applies to each of the three qualities:

- Customer centricity: In a customer-centered effort, this first stage assesses how an organization can attain competitive advantage with a greater knowledge of an attention to the needs of its customers—whether those customers are external to the organization or internal staff, like the clinic workers at ClinicCo.

- Operational excellence: When focusing on this quality, the company determines how operational improvements can contribute to the efficient operation of the enterprise by shifting teams to higher-value activities, as defined by its customers and strategy. The value comes from improving not just problems with one group or function, but efforts spanning functional areas of the business across the whole organization. At ClinicCo, the improvement needed to address everything from scheduling of nurses to provisioning of equipment to interactions with insurance companies so nurses could focus primarily on patient care. Unless everyone bought into the solution and moved forward together, the Scheduler tool could not generate the hoped-for improvements.

- Enterprise agility: The organization must determine where and how agility can create faster responses and more effectively address the changing needs of the business. These changes are about embracing the concept of constant, iterative, agile improvement, not a one-time, static solution. Agility pays off only if the organization proselytizes the idea of identifying and prioritizing the most crucial improvements and continually updating a road map to deliver on them.

It's not enough to simply identify the hoped-for value of the transformation. That value must be translated into a well-communicated vision that stakeholders can embrace as the organization moves through the challenge of a change. Communicating that vision, not just at the start, but throughout the process, is essential to keeping everyone moving in the right direction, regardless of their position or role in the organization.

Embrace an overarching philosophy of systems thinking

In every large organization, there is a yawning gap between strategy and reality. That's because big organizations are complex and interconnected systems of people, processes, and technology. You can't take a system like that and drag it into the future on nothing but hope—and you can't get there by making small and disconnected steps, even if each is a step in the right direction.

This is where systems thinking comes in. Systems thinking looks at the organization holistically, recognizing how groups and processes within the company interact with and influence each other. Those systems may be management departments, technology components, or entrenched ways of working. But true improvement that creates value can only happen when those attempting to move forward have recognized how their hoped-for contributions interact with the systems in the company.

For any organization, systems thinking must start from the needs of the customer and radiate out; it must embrace excellence in execution across all functions; and it must propel the agility of the enterprise. Here's how that systems thinking helped accelerate ClinicCo's transformation to a more responsive company.

- Customer centricity: A naive perspective would suggest that only the functions closest to customers, such as marketing, sales, or service, need customer-centric thinking. But every customer experience is connected to all of the systems in the company. At ClinicCo, systems thinking revealed that scheduling was central to the experience of both employees and patients. Improving the experience of employees contributed directly to improving the experience of patients.

- Operational excellence: The whole company must move forward together. This begins with an analysis of the operating model for the company and the development of a road map to improve it. Then you can identify where improved operations could increase the company's responsiveness and embrace improvements in that group, function, or process as part of the overall system of the company. At ClinicCo, this meant acknowledging that Scheduler would succeed only if it eventually embraced processes from equipment scheduling and staffing to patient onboarding and billing.

- Enterprise agility: Agile is not just a coding methodology. Enterprise agility means that every team making improvements must have representation across functions, so that each iterative step enables progress across the whole enterprise. The Agile development teams at ClinicCo succeeded because they regularly engaged with functional areas across the business such as operations, technology, finance, HR, and marketing to effectively prioritize work.

ClinicCo's solutions embraced systems including the clinics, the collection of insurance and public health rules it needed to comply with, the equipment it used, the technology systems used to schedule staff, the ways those staff communicated with management, the processes used to check patients in, the billing systems that ensured ClinicCo got paid, and so on. It was the interactions among all those systems that created the countless number of possible combinations that Scheduler needed to synergize—and the ultimate value of the operational solution.

Empower teams to improve skills and make decisions

As we described in chapter 1, change in the business world now happens so rapidly that top-down decision-making is ineffective. Unless the organization as a whole "knows" what its goal is and what it needs to do, it can't respond to opportunities.

If value creates the initial impetus and systems thinking the way to conceive the steps to the goal, then empowered teams are the atomic units of management that implement those steps.

For many companies, empowering teams is a cultural shift. Employees need to develop skills for customer centricity (identifying and executing on moments that matter), operational excellence (change management and decision-making), and enterprise agility (continuous learning). Here's how empowered teams made rapid improvements possible at ClinicCo:

- Customer centricity: Culturally, companies must shift from a world where every change requires review and approval to one where contributors don't need to ask permission to do what is right for customers. ClinicCo management recognized that scheduling was a crucial element of its ability to cope with and manage complexity and change. The team started out with an explicit charge to do what was necessary to solve the scheduling challenge.

- Operational excellence: Empowering teams requires people who can make smart decisions, which in turn demands building staff decision-making skills. It also requires a concerted change-management effort, so all contributors recognize the new way of working and buy into it. Because the improved Scheduler at ClinicCo touched so many parts of the company's business, its success depended on the intelligence and responsiveness of the clinic staff and managers adopting the application to complete their day-to-day responsibilities.

- Enterprise agility: The new way of working necessary for a responsive enterprise requires people to become comfortable with constant change and improvement. This works best when contributors develop a growth mindset, understanding that things not only can be better, but *should* be better, improving from week to week, month to month, and quarter to quarter. Every positive change that the Scheduler team made happened because the enterprise was ready to accept improvements throughout its business, from changing check-ins to improving hospital referrals.

At ClinicCo, the team that worked on Scheduler was fully empowered. The profundity of that development task might not be immediately obvious, but because it touched so many parts of ClinicCo's business, it could not be an off-to-the-side skunkworks project. The team working on it knew that the results of their work would change the way nearly everyone in the clinics did their jobs. Managers knew that what they were working on might upset some people, but in the end, it would get them closer to being efficient and safe with more time to focus on patient care.

A responsive company gives responsibility to the teams closest to the customers and the work that generates value. Those teams are most likely to be aware of what changes will make a powerful difference, as well as what problems are getting in the way of delivering value.

The teams will not seek permission to do the right things for the customer and the company. They will make mistakes, fail from time to time, and learn from those errors. That sounds dangerous, of course. But if a team understands where the value is coming from and how systems interact, it can make progress without having to follow a hundred steps in some senior manager's imagined action plan. It is leadership's responsibility to clear the way for teams, removing blockers that prevent rapid progress.

Embed feedback loops in systems and act on data

When any change happens in an enterprise, the fundamental question is, "Is it working?" Answering that question with any confidence requires measuring and acting on something that matters: generating data about revenues, profits, sales, costs, customer satisfaction, regulatory compliance, speed of operation, efficiency, and a hundred other possible metrics.

Another crucial quality of feedback loops is the democratization of data. Departments can no longer hoard data in silos. Successful companies aggregate data from functional areas of a business into centralized data visualization tools. Combining data from multiple sources surfaces previously unknown patterns and opportunities for improvement across areas of the business that do not always directly interact. Any empowered team must have access to any data source that will potentially allow it to measure success.

Taking action based on performance against a desired metric creates a closed loop in the transformation process. The vision in pursuit of value sets the general direction, systems thinking defines how to make progress, empowered teams work to deliver that progress, and feedback loops tell everyone whether the progress is actually happening, at what rate, and in what direction.

Feedback loops are central to all elements of the responsive enterprise transformation. You can't be customer-centric unless you have ways to measure progress; you can't find where operational excellence is and isn't working without data accessible to all that identifies gaps;

and you can't embrace enterprise agility unless you can rapidly measure whether changes are working. At ClinicCo, here's how feedback loops enabled rapid progress:

- Customer centricity: The time to identify success metrics is at the very start of each transformation effort. Those metrics might include anything from time to resolve customer problems to manufacturing defects, but each should trace back directly to improvements in customer experience. ClinicCo, Scheduler was instrumented to measure how quickly patients were served, how much downtime there was in equipment use, and levels of compliance—all crucial parts of creating an optimal experience for both patients and employees.

- Operational excellence: There must be more to measurement than "find a problem, then fix it." Instead, feedback loops create a comprehensive system for tracking and monitoring progress. The data they generate must be available to any department or function seeking to improve, so "We didn't know there was an issue" is no longer an excuse. Crucially, it shifts thinking from "Are we doing things right?" (efficiency) to "Are we doing the right things?" (effectiveness). Each efficiency that Scheduler introduced clarified other parts of the business that could potentially improve and other ways the tool could evolve to help.

- Enterprise agility: Enterprise agility requires a mindset of constant progress. That's virtually impossible without feedback loops. Companies must focus on short, immediate improvements rather than massive projects that pay off in the far future. That means implementing continuous feedback with data generated from tests and pilots, then quickly acting on that data. Scheduler was able to create growth and reduce waste in many aspects of ClinicCo's business because at each step along the way, feedback loops clarified what was working and opportunities for improvement.

The steps in the responsive transformation are no more than that—steps—without feedback loops. The loops dictate refinements to the vision, new ways to think about the systems, and new improvements the empowered teams can pursue. Closing those loops accelerates the enterprise's transformation to being responsive.

RESPONSIVENESS IS A TRANSFORMATION WORTH MAKING

One of the challenges with the concept of the responsive enterprise is that it is somewhat daunting. So companies may not start with the holistic idea of the responsive enterprise. Instead, they recognize an inefficiency that might be in the areas of customer centricity, operational excellence, or enterprise agility. But as the organization sees more value in these elements of responsiveness, the idea spreads throughout the organization. Eventually, the transformation becomes part of how the organization perceives itself: swifter, more efficient and responsive to changes in its environment, and more competitive.

As you can see from what happened at ClinicCo, the transformation into a responsive enterprise is an ongoing journey. And as should now be clear from the qualities we just described, customer centricity, operational excellence, and enterprise agility are interlocking goals. It's never enough to make progress on one dimension or another—a responsive enterprise makes progress on all of those goals at once. The mutual reinforcement that comes from that transformation is truly powerful. Everyone at the company begins to feel aligned and as if they are moving decisively and at a steady pace toward a common goal. And nothing— not even a global and unanticipated pandemic—can prevent them from reaching their goals.

In the rest of this book, we'll examine each of the three qualities of a responsive enterprise in detail, addressing the changes reflected in the columns of the transformation matrix. We'll also dive deeply into each of the four steps, examining how to succeed along the rows of the matrix. And we'll analyze the central role of technology, which can either solve problems or create impediments, depending on how you approach it. Taken together, these improvements contain everything you need to transform your company into a responsive enterprise.

Part II

QUALITIES OF THE RESPONSIVE ENTERPRISE

Chapter 3

CUSTOMER CENTRICITY AS A MOTIVATING PRINCIPLE

A large credit union, which we'll call CredCo, was serving eight million customers and had been rated the top bank for quality of customer experience for three years in a row. But banking is a competitive market, and banks and credit unions struggle to differentiate their mostly similar products and services. How could CredCo retain and grow its customer base?

CredCo's typical new customer is an eighteen-year-old with a modest income setting up banking for the first time. While such customers often live paycheck-to-paycheck, they mature to develop needs for financial products like credit cards, mortgages, and investments. They're susceptible to discount offers from other banks, so CredCo must invest in experiences that retain them as customers and grow their relationship with the organization.

All banks say they want to serve customers well. To differentiate, CredCo would need more than pride in customer service or lip-service to a customer-centric ideal. Its senior management realized that the company needed a program to identify and resolve the root causes of customer challenges, especially when those challenges crossed functional boundaries within the organization.

So CredCo created a dedicated digital innovation lab and tapped a manager with more than a decade of experience at the credit union to lead it. The lab included staff at various levels of seniority from departments like customer service, technology, branch operations, legal, product development, and compliance. And the lab reported directly to the CEO. This structure ensured it could identify real customer problems and conceive solutions that would require coordinated change from multiple functional areas.

To start the lab on its mission, the credit union identified a particularly annoying issue for customers: vendor disputes.

Imagine that you are a customer or spouse living on a tight budget. You notice a debit card charge on your bill that doesn't belong there—for example, a vendor who has billed you twice, a charge from a merchant that never delivered the product, or an additional fee that you didn't authorize. So you contact the credit union and attempt to get that charge removed.

Such disputes were costly not just for the customers but also for the credit union, which had to dedicate resources in both customer service and back-office operations to track down and resolve the problems. Disputes could take weeks to resolve, generating mail correspondence to customers that was so delayed that the customers receiving it might have forgotten the original dispute. And the challenge wasn't just cost: if the credit union failed to resolve such disputes in a timely and effective way, it could be subject to penalties and fines from regulators.

CredCo had attempted to streamline the process multiple times before. But this time would be different.

To start, the participants in the digital lab would tackle the problem from the customer's perspective. What would a customer want to happen? What was getting in the way of delivering that? What departments and functions were involved, and how could the credit union make changes in those functions that would streamline solving the dispute?

The digital lab used analytics to identify dispute patterns. For example, about 30% of the disputes fit a pattern that was nearly always resolved in the customer's favor. The lab piloted a solution that automated resolving such problems, reducing the resolution time from months or weeks down to milliseconds. This not only made the customers happier; it also saved time for both customer service and back-office resources.

The lab identified similar ways to streamline the resolution of other disputes, including applying behavioral science to redesign the online form used to report charges. The solutions cut across functions, requiring the web group to revise online functionality, customer service to retrain its reps, IT to update the systems those reps used, and back-office operations to change its dispute resolution process.

The pilot rollout generated measurable improvements in metrics like reducing time to resolve disputes, reducing customer service resource demand, and reducing load on back-office functions. So CredCo moved to roll it out across its entire system.

This was just the first of many successes for the lab. The next challenge was to improve the process for credit card applications. The goal here was not just making it easier to apply for a credit card. It was also getting customers to use it once they were approved. Like many consumers, CredCo credit card holders often had multiple cards; what would it take to get the CredCo card to be "top of wallet"?

Customer research revealed that the speed of approval was only part of the problem. Customers wanted instant access to the card, *before* it arrived in the mail. So the lab piloted Digital Card Issuance, or DCI, delivering an instant virtual digital card via email. Again, the success was dramatic and measurable: customers with instant digital access to cards increased their credit card use by 200% over the first thirty days.

Another success, which we'll describe in more detail in chapter 10, was reengineering the process to increase approvals for increasing the size of loans. The lab combined user experience testing and content strategy to overhaul the decision process, combining seven disparate systems into one and streamlining communication between departments. The result was far quicker decisions when customers had an immediate, or even desperate, need for capital.

The lab did its job: changing how CredCo thinks about customers. The company has since replicated and propagated similar customer-focused, cross-functional teams across the enterprise and invested heavily in data intelligence and insights to power those teams. Because that work overrides considerations in departmental silos, the credit union can find ways to serve demanding customers with ideas that other banks find hard to copy. And in the competitive world of mostly similar banking experiences, that's what keeps CredCo's customer base happy and growing.

WHY CUSTOMER EXPERIENCE MATTERS

Banking is not the only market where competitors struggle to differentiate. In the past 100 years, we have witnessed innovation on a massive scale. Initially, innovation results in clear market leaders, but eventually competitors catch up and product parity becomes the norm.

For the most part now, phones are phones, washing machines are washing machines, medical treatment is medical treatment. Suppliers can compete on price, but that tends to favor only the largest player in a market. They can try to build other barriers to competition, such as filing for patents. But when the playing field is level, an unwavering commitment to customer experience (CX) generates durable brand value and true differentiation that's very hard to compete with. That's why CredCo keeps growing. And it's why any company that makes a serious, long-term investment in CX can do the same, even in an otherwise undifferentiated market.

Companies are beginning to understand this. Among the 418 business decision-makers in the Forrester Consulting study we described in chapter 1, 86% said, "Finding ways to be more customer-centric in our decisions" was a high priority, and 41% agreed that it was among their top priorities.

There's a reason for this commitment to customer centricity: It tends to generate profits. The American Customer Satisfaction Index (ACSI) has been studying this for years, and its data proves the value of a better customer experience. ACSI constructed a stock portfolio from a weighted combination of the top thirty to thirty-five companies in each industry based on the organization's proprietary customer satisfaction research.[6] It adjusted the makeup of the portfolio quarterly based on customer experience scores. Over the period from 2006 to 2021, the annualized return of the ACSI Leaders portfolio was 17.3%, compared with a 9.0% annual return on the S&P 500 over the same time period (see figure 3-1).

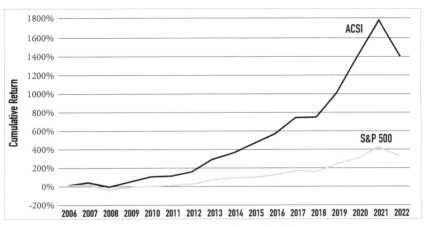

Figure 3-1. Customer experience leaders generate superior stock performance.
Source: ACSI

Customer experience is an investment, and it pays off much more consistently than other investments such as advertising and acquisitions. A better customer experience translates to a differentiation that customers notice. Differentiation feeds the brand. It retains customers even in fiercely competitive environments. And it encourages customers to maintain and grow the relationship. That's a value that generates growth in good economic times and resilience in more challenging periods. When companies continually come through for you, you stick with them.

It also generates word of mouth. Here's one example. In 2012, the family of Chris Hurn, CEO of Fountainhead, stayed at the Ritz-Carlton resort in Amelia Island, Florida.[7] Hurn's young son had a beloved stuffed giraffe named Joshie. When the family returned from Florida, Joshie was missing. Hurn's son was inconsolable—he settled down only when Hurn told him that Joshie was "taking an extra-long vacation at the resort."

When Hurn contacted the Ritz-Carlton, the staff told him they had discovered Joshie in the laundry. Hurn explained how distraught his son had become, and the staff at the Ritz assured him they'd take care of it.

Soon a package arrived at Hurn's home from the resort. Inside was not just Joshie, but a binder of photos showing the stuffed giraffe lounging by the pool in sunglasses, getting a massage at the spa with cucumbers on his eyes, relaxing in a comfy chair with other plush toys, and "driving" a golf cart at the beach.

The point here is not that somebody at the Ritz-Carlton did something nice. It's that the Ritz-Carlton had, and maintains, a culture of service excellence across all touchpoints of its brand. Of course the staff at Amelia Island would find a way to showcase that service for a customer. The Ritz-Carlton maintains a premium price because of its service reputation for exceptional experience. And the story of Joshie the Giraffe has spread that legendary reputation, now mentioned on 123,000 web pages.

THE TEST FOR CUSTOMER-CENTRIC IMPROVEMENTS

There is a fundamental tension at the center of all customer-centric efforts within companies. After all, what customers typically want is *everything*, and they don't want to pay a lot for it. That's clearly not a viable way for a company to succeed.

To decide just how far to go in serving customers, a customer-centric company must consider changes that share three qualities: they are desirable, feasible, and viable (see figure 3-2).[8] Improvements in customer experience happen at the intersection of these three qualities.

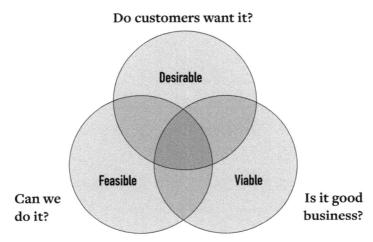

Do customers want it?

Figure 3-2. The three qualities of a workable customer experience improvement.
Source: IDEO

- A **desirable** offering is one that the customer wants. You can assess this quality by asking if a significant group of customers would find the offering better than what they're getting now, for example, because it is cheaper, faster, more enjoyable, or more dependable.

- A **feasible** offering is one that is possible to deliver. You can assess this quality by determining how your current operations would have to change to deliver the offering. Would you need to retrain staff or rework technology? Or would you have to scrap and rebuild whole parts of your business? The former is feasible, while the latter is not.

- A **viable** offering is one that generates growth or profit, and therefore is good for the business. Giving your product away is generally not viable—at least for the long term. But bundling it into another profitable offering may be, as may be providing a free trial period.

Consider how this framework applied at a massive medical and health company that is one of the largest US companies by revenue. The company, which we'll call HealthCo, has begun a transformation in customer-centric improvements. The company's senior director of digital experience and design, "Marge," recognized that the key to getting that transformation started was to choose a single company in the company's portfolio as a starting point and build on successes at that company.

In 2010, HealthCo had acquired a network of cancer treatment centers that treats almost a million patients a year. To identify where patient experience could improve, we worked with the cancer treatment centers to review the entire end-to-end experience of a cancer patient. Patients interacted with nineteen different staff roles. We reviewed the process at five different treatment centers.

A study of the processes revealed that the clearest opportunity for improvement was the intake process. It often took two to four weeks between the referral to the clinic and the patient's first appointment, at which point the patient might meet with multiple staff in different roles. Workers at the cancer centers were dedicated and empathetic, but were saddled with a need to use disparate software applications, cutting and pasting information in a time-consuming process to get the intake prepared. Given the stress and anxiety that a cancer diagnosis generates, these delays led to about 40% of patients failing to initiate or to complete their treatment at the cancer center.

The cancer treatment centers' intake process fits the three criteria for a promising potential customer experience improvement. It was clearly desirable to streamline the process so that patients could go quickly from diagnosis to referral to treatment. Reengineering systems to ease the process for intake staffers was feasible, since it required only changes in software systems, rather than changing medical treatment. And a change that decreased the number of patients who gave up would be a highly viable improvement, since a typical patient averages $40,000 to $70,000 of treatment bills during a course of treatment.

As we write this, HealthCo has begun piloting the cancer center improvements. And it will use this change as a template for change elsewhere in the broader company to change the culture and identify places where desirable, feasible, viable customer experience improvements could have the greatest impact.

When an organization like CredCo or HealthCo empowers a cross-functional team to pursue customer-centric innovation, this triad of customer-experience elements is constantly on the mind of those innovators. Customer journey mapping and customer research identify the moments that matter most to customers, patients, or clients and opportunities to secure brand loyalty. Working across functions expands the boundaries of what is feasible. Keeping the economics in mind, testing the innovations to see how customers react and analyzing quantitative data determine if the results are truly viable in the long term.

Turning a corporate value of customer centricity into an effective competitive advantage takes major effort. Let's look at three elements of that effort: organizing for customer centricity, implementing customer-centric practices, and innovating solutions with design thinking.

ORGANIZING AND MANAGING FOR CUSTOMER CENTRICITY

While companies hope to serve customers well, they don't always achieve that goal. In the Forrester Consulting study of business decision-makers that we mentioned earlier, only 36% of respondents agreed that their company consistently meets, delivers on, or exceeds customers' needs and expectations (see figure 3-3). And only 16% said their ability to identify and respond to customer needs had significantly improved.

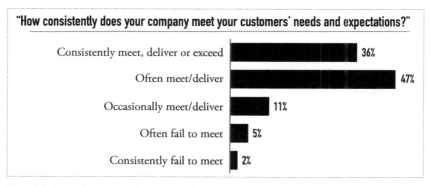

"How consistently does your company meet your customers' needs and expectations?"

Consistently meet, deliver or exceed	36%
Often meet/deliver	47%
Occasionally meet/deliver	11%
Often fail to meet	5%
Consistently fail to meet	2%

Figure 3-3. A minority of companies consistently meet or exceed consumer needs.
Source: A commissioned study conducted by Forrester Consulting on behalf of Celerity, November 2021. Base: 418 North American digital strategy decision-makers.

How must a company change to enable it to act on customer experience insights? Starting an innovation lab or center of excellence, as CredCo did, is helpful but not sufficient. The key is to set up the organizational frameworks that transform a desire to serve customers better into actual action:

- **Define a CX vision.** The commitment to customer experience starts at the top. Senior managers must create a compelling description of an ideal future state that the company is working together to achieve. The vision should be simple to describe (for example, "We respond more quickly to customer needs than any competitor" or "We ensure that our customers can get effective service in any channel"). Leaders must then use regular and consistent corporate messaging, training, and incentives to help the entire workforce to embrace and act on the vision and then hold people accountable.

- **Define CX strategy.** CX strategy aligns corporate initiatives toward a common goal of improving CX. Once a company defines the vision, the year-to-year strategy must acknowledge how each initiative will improve customer experiences and generate higher degrees of customer satisfaction and loyalty. But CX strategy is no more than words on a page unless budgets follow CX priorities.

- **Promote a CX mindset.** Every role in the company can contribute to customer experience. Workers in customer service, marketing, and product development may initially understand this better than people in IT, human resources, or finance, but unless a CX mindset prevails throughout the company, progress will be slow and uneven. As CredCo learned, back-office functions were just as essential to making customer improvements as customer touchpoints like apps, retail branches, and call centers. Companies with a CX mindset understand that even everyday transactions like sending an invoice are opportunities to create a positive experience.

- **Improve CX collaboration.** Departmental silos are where CX improvements go to die. Fixing that means building frameworks that enable functions to share in identifying CX problems, designing solutions, and implementing those solutions. A design lab like CredCo's can get things started, but in a fully functional customer-centric organization, collaborating on and solving CX problems becomes part of everyone's everyday work. When the value of the CX changes becomes clear, it becomes a thread that is woven into how everyone works together.

- **Implement CX measurement.** CX improvement efforts will falter unless everyone—especially senior leaders—has visibility into what's working and what's not. That means an investment in regular CX metrics and key performance indicators (KPIs), shared broadly across the company. According to Harley Manning and Kerry Bodine's seminal CX book *Outside In: The Power of Putting Customers at the Center of Your Business,* such metrics should align with how customers judge experiences and must be consistent across channels and lines of business. Metrics include subjective measures, such as consumer survey responses and Net Promoter Scores, along with quantitative measures like service call volume, time to resolve problems, churn, and growth. Dashboards of such measures should be shared broadly internally, and managers should regularly refer to them.

- **Define CX governance.** Governance answers each department and function's fundamental question: "What's my job with respect to customers?" Role descriptions should reflect how each department contributes and what it's responsible for. And crucially, CX governance must also include compensation rewards and penalties associated with contributing to overall customer-centricity goals.

The Forrester Consulting survey of business decision-makers asked whether companies had the measurement and governance tools in place to deliver on these CX promises. About four out of five said they did. For example, 86% agreed that they had systems in place to continuously assess the value they deliver to customers, and 84% continuously track, report, and respond to the relationship between customer success or experience and their business performance (see figure 3-4).

IMPLEMENTING CUSTOMER-CENTRIC PRACTICES

Organizing and managing for customer experience creates energy from the top down. But nothing can change unless the enterprise invests in tools that staff can use to implement CX practices. In the Forrester Consulting survey of business decision-makers, 85% planned a moderate or significant investment in meeting customer demand and expectations, and 80% planned such investments in understanding customers' changing needs and preferences (see figure 3-5).

"How much do you agree with the following statements?"

■ Agree ■ Strongly Agree

We have a system in place/feedback mechanisms (external and internal) to continuously assess the value we are delivering to our customers — **49%** | **37%** | **86%**

We have a strategy in place to continuously adapt our people, processes, and technology strategy in an uncertain business environment — **52%** | **33%** | **86%**

We are able to support our employees with the tools and processes they need to succeed for both in-office and remote work — **45%** | **40%** | **86%**

We continuously track, report, and respond to the relationship between customer success/experience and our business performance — **45%** | **39%** | **84%**

We can effectively translate and combine our data pools into actionable insights — **43%** | **40%** | **83%**

We can translate customer data insights into smarter decisions driving operational execution in an effective, agile manner — **48%** | **34%** | **82%**

We have the right set of digital capabilities (internally and externally) in place to help deliver value to our customers — **46%** | **35%** | **82%**

We have established a culture that puts customer experience and success at the heart of everything we do — **42%** | **39%** | **81%**

Figure 3-4. Most companies have systems to monitor delivery on CX promises.
Source: A commissioned study conducted by Forrester Consulting on behalf of Celerity, November 2021. Base: 418 North American digital strategy decision-makers. Percentages may not sum to total shown due to rounding.

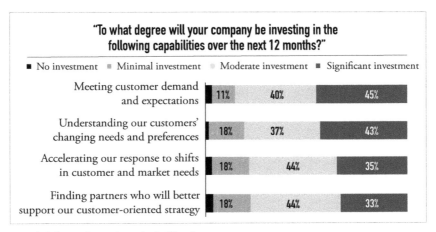

Figure 3–5. Companies are investing in CX tools.
Source: A commissioned study conducted by Forrester Consulting on behalf of Celerity, November 2021. Base: 418 North American digital strategy decision-makers.

Here's a list of the tools most necessary for efforts to improve customer experience.

- **Customer research.** This includes a regular program of voice-of-the-customer research that identifies what's working, what's not, and where improvements are possible. Such programs include both survey responses and regular focus groups or interviews to get at qualitative insights. Companies can also learn from interviewing frontline employees and conducting ethnographic research—obtaining selected customers' permission to observe them in their homes or in retail stores. A customer research group should regularly document the results of these efforts, including defining customer personas and internally publishing research insights.

- **Journey mapping and service design.** Intense, cross-functional journey mapping exercises reveal root causes of customer problems, which makes them an essential activity for starting to solve those problems. In a journey mapping workshop, participants across functions identify the steps consumers take in interacting with a company, the workers who must serve them, the systems that the workers use, and so on, tracing back problems to underlying causes several steps back. For example, HealthCo found that challenges with onboarding patients at its cancer clinics had their roots in the multiple systems and processes underlying the admission process. Journey mapping is one of the systems thinking tools we describe in chapter 7.

- **Priority scoring.** Not all CX problems are equal. A crucial part of CX strategy and execution is prioritizing the problems that have the greatest impact on customers and value delivery—the moments that matter. This exercise defines benefits and costs for the desirable/feasible/viable framework to help determine what the company should actually work on.

- **Personalization.** The path to better customer experience frequently depends on effective digital service. Companies typically know a lot about the customer they're serving, but do they use that information to make things easier? Anyone who's had to explain the same information to three successive service reps on the same call knows how companies' inability to effectively use customer information generates frustration, anger, and ultimately lost business. Conversely, intelligently designed digital experiences can use personal data to delight customers with exactly the help and services they need, anticipating the moment when the company can be most helpful.

- **Data and analytics.** Data is the fuel for customer experience. Analyzing the flow of data through systems often generates fruitful insights for CX improvements. Smart analysis of data also shows where people are getting stuck and having problems, a discipline known as customer journey analytics. Data also enables predictive analytics, a method that looks at patterns in customer behavior and anticipates, based on each customer's past experiences, what they're most likely to want to do next.

- **Future mapping.** Customer experience is not just about giving people what they want; it's about figuring out what they *will* want. Charlene Li's book *The Disruption Mindset: Why Some Organizations Transform while Others Fail* posits that all disruption fundamentally comes from enterprises' inability to anticipate the changing needs of their customers. For example, this kind of thinking is what allowed the financial services firm USAA to invent mobile check deposits, saving customers from having to take trips to the bank. Future mapping redefines what is feasible, enabling advances that will keep competitors in the rear-view mirror.

INNOVATING SOLUTIONS WITH DESIGN THINKING

The right organization and tools will make innovation possible. But how do you actually design the solution to a problem? One way to generate the most imaginative solutions to problems is with design thinking, an idea pioneered by Herbert A. Simon in 1969 and refined and popularized by the leading design firm IDEO in the 1990s.[9]

Design thinking starts with the desirability/viability/feasibility framework that we described near the start of this chapter. That lens allows innovators to identify the right problems to solve. From there, the process can go forward in a series of iterative steps. For example, here's how IDEO defines the steps in design thinking:[10]

1. **Frame a question.** Identify a driving question that inspires others to search for creative solutions.

2. **Gather inspiration.** Inspire new thinking by discovering what people really need.

3. **Generate ideas.** Push past obvious solutions to get to breakthrough ideas.

4. **Make ideas tangible.** Build rough prototypes to learn how to make ideas better.

5. **Test to learn.** Refine ideas by gathering feedback and experimenting forward.

6. **Share the story.** Craft a human story to inspire others toward action.

How does that process work in practice? Aaron Kennelly, our VP of CX, advocates learning by doing in our design workshops. In these sessions, we engage stakeholders from multiple departments in a five-day sprint. On the first day, we work with everyone to align on challenges worth investment and sketch a variety of possible solutions. On day two, we vote to decide on the best solutions and use storyboarding to define a prototype. On the third day, we design and build that prototype and recruit some users to test it. Day four is for user testing; we get qualitative feedback from the testers, typically about five people who stand in for actual customers. And, finally, we create a report about the project, assembling assets and making recommendations on how to move forward from prototype to pilot project.

Notice a few qualities about this method. It starts from what the customer needs, not from what the company wants. It is tempered by an analysis of feasibility (to make sure we are designing something possible) and viability (to prove that the results, if successful, will actually benefit the business). It is a lightweight process that values speed over perfection. It fosters cross-functional collaboration. And it structures future conversations, framing them to be about problems and solutions: a fundamentally customer-centric perspective.

Note that the sprint alone won't solve a problem. But it points the way to a solution. The next step is to build an actual pilot project, tying it in with all the various affected functions (for example, website, app, back-end databases, approval processes, customer service systems, and training) so that it is actually functional for customers. The team then tests it with a subset of customers, gathers data, and refines the project based on that feedback (or cancels it, if it turns out not to be viable after all).

This is a fundamentally Agile process. Design sprints are fast and low-risk. They increase the likelihood of success and reduce the risk profile of pilot projects. The pilots can launch quickly, and if the organization has set up metrics properly, the team can rapidly determine if they're worthy of a broader rollout that would benefit a large segment of the customer base.

HOW CUSTOMER CENTRICITY PERVADES AN ORGANIZATION

As we described in the previous chapter, the changes an enterprise moves through proceed in four steps: expose value, embrace systems thinking, empower teams, and embed feedback loops. Here's how those steps apply to customer centricity.

Clearly exposing value is essential for changing mindsets

Leaders must develop a clear vision for how investments in customer centricity will benefit the organization. That analysis should start with a foundation of customer research to expose where you can create more value. Then use this to inform the organization's priorities and its strategy.

This clear description of value, and the mindset that follows from it, are like the soil in which customer centricity will grow. Unless leaders expose the value, engage their managers, and train the staff—and continually reinforce the mindset in the way they communicate management decisions—customer centricity will be no more than a slogan.

Systems thinking is what makes customer-centric innovation possible

What affects the customer experience? Everything. The speed of response of an IT staffer, the hiring process used by HR, the level of flexibility of a legal team, or the willingness to shift priorities in marketing: all may end up as necessary components of a customer-centric shift.

It's no coincidence that every part of customer-centric change crosses organizational functions. It's not possible for a company to become customer-centric unless every function and department buys in. It's this level of systems thinking that enables not just innovation, but also sustained commitment to collaborate on improving customer experience in the moments that matter.

Empowered teams generate change

Change at CredCo accelerated when the cross-functional team in the digital innovation lab began inventing new ways to serve customers. This is a typical way that change starts: a center of excellence or a pilot team comes together to use design thinking to invent new ways to improve the customer experience.

In more mature organizations, such teams are everywhere. Because the lines of communication among departments are always open, there are far more opportunities to make change happen. Task forces, prototyping groups, and even random conversations generate more ideas—and teams that can implement them are a common occurrence. This is what happens when customer centricity becomes everyone's job: the enterprise builds a culture where it's not necessary to ask permission to do the right thing.

Of the business decision-makers in the Forrester Consulting survey, two-thirds agreed that doing the right thing for the customer in their companies was more important than adhering to established tasks and processes and that they ensure that employees are empowered with technology and insights to help create value for customers. This is certainly the idea. But attaining it in practice requires difficult decisions that not all companies are ready to make.

Feedback loops are essential for customer-centric change

All customer-centric processes require data and feedback to succeed. Customer research shows where the problems are. Design sprints demand user tests to build better prototypes. Pilots move forward based on measuring what's working and reviewing data from customer journey analytics.

More broadly, the enterprise itself shifts its work based on customer metrics. Improvements in customer satisfaction and Net Promoter Scores prove out the customer-centric philosophy. And detailed analysis of where customers are satisfied and where they are not points the way toward shifts in strategy and budget.

CUSTOMER CENTRICITY IS PART OF A BROADER TRANSFORMATION

A customer-centric organization has its priorities straight. But for it to act effectively on those priorities, it must develop the skills of operational excellence and enterprise agility. That's what we describe in the next two chapters.

Chapter 4

OPERATIONAL EXCELLENCE AS AN ESSENTIAL VIRTUE

Imagine a group of 1,500 technology development staff working across two geographies half a world apart. Now imagine telling all of those people that they need to adopt a new way of working to improve the company's efficiency and responsiveness.

That's the major challenge that a man we'll call "Bruce," a vice president at a large global retailer, RetailCo, faced in early 2021. Bruce was responsible for the company's financial technology (fintech) platforms. RetailCo had a well-deserved reputation for maximizing efficiency with decisions based on hard data. Bruce's finance technology group was responsible for supplying that data; nearly every decision any buyer or strategist within the company made touched the group's technology.

Bruce's ultimate objective was to make his group's technology more responsive to the needs of its customers. That included its internal customers—employees in RetailCo's business operations. By giving those employees quicker and more accurate information from the fintech group, this change would also improve the company's responsiveness to the expectations of its ultimate customers, the shoppers in its stores. Bruce would also be aligning his group's working methods with the rest of RetailCo's technology groups, which were moving in an increasingly Agile direction.

Fundamentally, the organization would shift from its functional focus on projects and systems to a mindset focused on capabilities and products. By structuring its work as the creation and refinement of products, the fintech group could align itself more with the demands most relevant for the business.

Central to this shift was a team structure called "Four in the Box." Each team would have four leads with complementary responsibilities. The business lead would focus on the goals of the business ("Why are we doing this?"). The design lead would focus on the user experience ("How does it feel to use this?"). The product lead would focus on the vision for the product ("What are we building?"). And the engineering lead would focus on the actual development plan ("How are we building this?"). While it might seem counterintuitive that this four-headed team could be efficient, the four leads balance the team's efforts based both on what was desirable and what was feasible, enabling steady incremental progress for each product.

Working toward a common goal, these cross-functional teams could respond more quickly to the needs of their internal customers. And they would empower employees to proactively identify problems to solve and iterate toward solutions. As employees took more initiative, they would gain broad and diverse experience and have a better path forward in their careers.

Our job was to partner with Bruce to design and execute the rollout of this shift. This work started with a big push to define and communicate the vision behind the change. Bruce prepared high-level messaging. Working with his nine top leaders both in the US and India, he explained how the product-led organization would better serve the fintech group's internal customers, reduce waste and political wrangling, and create a consistent framework for progress based on the Four-in-the-Box model.

We worked with RetailCo's leaders to think carefully about how to roll out the new structure. In particular, we did a RASCI analysis of the Four-in-the-Box roles, defining which roles were responsible, accountable, supporting, consulted, or informed of all areas of responsibility for each project. This helped everyone to understand where they fit and what work they would need to do.

Since there would soon be more than fifty teams working on various products throughout the fintech group, this rollout demanded extensive training, starting with Bruce's nine top leaders and moving on to all the individual employees who would participate. That training happened in

May of 2022, just three short months after the project began. Central to the training project was a TED-style talk evangelizing the new Four-in-the-Box structure.

Moving forward quickly was essential. In the absence of detailed and accurate information about the shift, misinformation and noise could interfere with the message; people tend to become apprehensive about changes they don't fully understand. Throughout June, July, August, and September, leadership continued regular biweekly communication, ran group-level workshops, continued to provide information to the full team, and listened and responded to concerns from Bruce's global leaders.

You can't make a change like this without monitoring what's happening with carefully designed metrics. So the team used surveys to monitor how many employees were aware of the shift, how many were committed to it, how many were proficient in the necessary skills, and how many were actually using the Four-in-the-Box principles. Awareness and commitment levels remain high and growing, and skill proficiency continues to increase.

There was plenty of uncertainty involved in the shift, but that's to be expected in any major change in a group this size. As we are writing this, though, RetailCo's fintech group has made significant progress. Adoption of the ideas has now reached 100% of all the employees surveyed, and proficiency is at 85%. The group is on the threshold of realizing the performance gains of the new, more responsive model. That's a meaningful operational improvement, because the adoption of a product mindset was essential to enable rapid and continuous improvement to serve the group's internal customers.

RESPONSIVENESS MEANS NOT JUST DOING THINGS RIGHT, BUT ALSO DOING THE RIGHT THINGS

If the world would stand still for a while, you could just build the most efficient company possible for that static world. Workers would do their jobs in the most efficient way possible, and managers would manage the company in the most efficient way possible. For much of the twentieth century, this was in fact how well-managed companies competed.

But the world now is in constant motion. It never stands still. That means a well-managed company must do more than do everything right. It must do the right things—and which things are appropriate can shift from quarter to quarter. Strategy in the twenty-first century is dynamic, changing from year to year and month to month to adapt to changes in market conditions, whether that means a rise in new competitors, a shift in consumer demand, or disruptions in the business environment from new technology tools and channels.

That shifting environment demands a new method of management. Just as RetailCo's fintech group needed to change the way it operated, so must any enterprise in today's dynamic business environment.

For enterprises, responsiveness includes the ability to maintain the delivery of value in changing conditions. It's not enough to have a flexible and adaptive strategy. Companies must embrace practices that enable efficient execution of that dynamic and changeable strategy. And that's a problem. In the Forrester Consulting survey of business decision-makers that we described in chapter 1, one in three said that lack of coordination across teams or organizations was a significant barrier to responding to change. And one in five said that at their companies, groups like IT, marketing, and product management weren't good at collaborating across functions.

Effective management matters more than ever. The business school professors Raffaella Sadun, Nicholas Bloom, and John Van Reenen spent a decade studying the value of effective management with a data set of 12,000 firms. As they wrote in *Harvard Business Review*, even though people imagine that management processes are just table stakes, "Firms with strong managerial processes do significantly better on high-level metrics such as profitability, growth, and productivity."[11] And response to change is at the center of this differentiation. "Just as the ability to discern competitive shifts is important to firm performance, so too is the ability to make sure that operational effectiveness is truly part of the organization's DNA," they write.

How can you manage effectively in an environment characterized by change? You must align your people, processes, and technology to be more efficient and receptive to what employee and customer needs are. That includes innovation in anticipation of what future customer needs, challenges, and pain points might be, including the needs of younger generations of customers with higher expectations or implicit needs that the customers cannot even articulate yet. Responsive enterprises are constantly looking for gaps in their operational effectiveness and opportunities to operate more efficiently. This includes, for example:

- Improving delivery to customers in terms of speed, cost, or value.
- Lowering costs by improving productivity or integrating acquisitions.
- Effectively predicting market changes and shifting customer requirements.
- Scaling the business by hiring smartly, improving processes, and modernizing and integrating systems for smoother interoperation.
- Elevating workers' effectiveness by reducing turnover, improving skills, or helping people adapt to change.

Changes like this eliminate friction and align resources appropriately to opportunities for the business. They increase productivity and accelerate decision-making. They turn the business into a machine that doesn't have to trade off efficiency with responsiveness—that is, an enterprise that can embrace and thrive on change.

ORGANIZATIONAL CHANGE MANAGEMENT IS ESSENTIAL FOR ALL SUCH TRANSFORMATIONS

Remaking organizations to be more operationally effective is challenging, like any corporate transformation. Profound change is often necessary for any operational improvement. But as much as people protest that they want to make changes, organizational change is difficult because it challenges established habits and ways of working. Or as Scott Adams' Dilbert cleverly articulated it: "Change is good. You go first."

This is why the discipline of organizational change management exists. Creating and establishing new ways of working is a matter of more than changing behavior. It demands a change in mindset, leading to a change in habits. Only when the mindset and habits change will the change stick.

Leaders know that change is hard. In the Forrester Consulting survey of business decision-makers, 30% cited inadequate organizational change management capabilities as a barrier to their responsiveness.

Chip Heath and Dan Heath point out in their book *Switch: How to Change Things When Change Is Hard* that every change brings up a conflict in our brains. The rational mind may understand the logic behind the needed change, but the emotional mind loves the comfort of the existing routine and resists the effort required. Organizationally speaking, change happens when you engage both sides of the mind. You must demonstrate how change will benefit everyone, and then you must design a system to establish habits that make it emotionally easier to change and harder to resist.

There is a pattern to all organizational change management efforts, whether they're the adoption of Four-in-the-Box structure at Retail-Co's fintech group, or embracing human-centered design at CreditCo, or getting merged companies to adopt a common way of working. The mandate for change comes from a senior executive, such as a CEO, president, COO, or chief customer officer. For changes that affect smaller

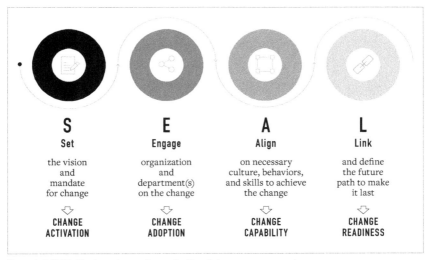

Figure 4-1. SEAL: The four stages of organizational change management.
Source: Celerity

groups, the mandate typically comes from the head of the group. With the help of a team, that executive defines a vision and continues with engaging the organization, aligning behaviors, and addressing the inevitable adoption challenges. Rebecca Sweda, our VP of operational excellence, describes it using the acronym SEAL, which reminds everyone of the four steps (see figure 4-1):[12]

- **Set** the vision and mandate for change (change activation). In this stage, the leaders of the organization define the desired future state, set out the desired goals, clarify the need for change, and identify the specific processes, roles, systems, and structures that must change in the organization or department. This stage succeeds when the leaders define a clear and compelling case for change and obtain buy-in from their top tier of leaders. At

RetailCo's fintech group, this stage involved a clear case for how the Four-in-the-Box organizational structure would enable the group to be more responsive to its internal customers' needs.

- **Engage** the organization and departments on the change (change adoption). This is where change begins to take hold. The top tier of leaders begins to address what actually must change and where resistance may come from. They develop a plan to cascade the case for change across the organization. And they identify what gaps in the organization's capabilities might block or slow the change. This stage succeeds when the leaders are ready to drive the change across the organization. At RetailCo, this stage included gaining the active support of the top nine leaders in the US and India and doing the RASCI analysis for the Four-in-the-Box roles.

- **Align** on the necessary culture, behavior, and skills to achieve the change (change capability). This is where the change spreads throughout the organization. Leaders identify the new knowledge and skills needed and the best ways to model and embed the required behaviors. They determine if and how culture may need to change and what it will take to get people to commit. This stage succeeds when leaders can create commitment, close capability gaps, and eliminate old and counterproductive behaviors. At RetailCo, this stage included training the majority of staff and organizing a slew of new responsive cross-functional teams to manage and improve the newly productized financial systems.

- **Link** with and define the future path to make it stick and make it last (change readiness). In this stage, the leaders identify how to address and remediate the inevitable challenges that arise. They develop methods to codify and spread lessons learned. They work on maintaining urgency as the change progresses and embedding the vision into the organization's day-to-day activities. This stage succeeds when the organization has effectively made itself responsible for embedding the vision into day-to-day work and can measure that progress. At RetailCo, this stage was visible in the high levels of adoption and proficiency as the group did an increasing amount of its work in the new structure.

At each of these stages, it's essential to measure progress. For example, at the first stage of setting the vision, organizations can measure awareness and support among staff, and when going forward into engagement, they can measure proficiency and skill gaps. In the alignment stage, they can measure capability gaps addressed and commitment among stakeholders. In the linking stage, they can measure whether the new behaviors are observed and how people respond to detailed surveys about the change.

This systematic organizational change management framework is essential for ensuring success in every transformation, especially those involved in establishing operational excellence. Organizational change management is how a strategic initiative is translated into effective execution.

In the rest of this chapter, we examine some specific types of transformations that can improve operational excellence: operating models and operational road maps, governance and measurement, and data and analytics.

OPERATING MODELS AND OPERATIONAL ROAD MAPS DEFINE A PATH TO OPERATIONAL EXCELLENCE

A first step in implementing change that will improve operational excellence is to create a visualization of how your company operates, identify how it could operate better in the future, and provide a road map from the current state to the future state.

Start with a current operating model: a visual representation of how your company delivers value to your customers. More sophisticated than the value chain diagrams of the past, the operating model captures how you deliver value: not just what you make and how you make it, but what is outsourced, what partners you work with, how departments and functions contribute, what systems are involved, what processes you use, how you manage everything, and how you measure and report on the results. The creation of such a model typically requires interviews with senior executives to gain clarity on the delivery of value in your organization.

Once you've done the exercise of mapping all of that out, you can assess what could be better. For example, how might you change the model to meet the needs of customers more responsively? What processes could work more smoothly and respond to change more quickly?

How could you shift reporting relationships and metrics to create an organization that is more responsive? Taken together, these changes allow you to describe a future operating model for your organization, one that is better suited to transform change into competitive advantage.

To get to that desired future state, the next step is to create an operational road map. The road map identifies and then sets out to correct gaps between a company's current state and desired future state.

To create the road map, the company must define measurable business objectives linked to the methods it uses to create value. Organizations must refine this with the goals needed to accomplish a specific strategy and KPIs that will indicate the progress toward that goal.

Next, a company must identify areas of opportunity, like RetailCo's desire to make its fintech systems more responsive. As with the future operating model, this is informed by interviews, conversations, and in-person observation to obtain a clear understanding of the current situation and identification of gaps between the current state and the desired future state. The result of this analysis is to identify the teams, processes, content, and technologies that can be improved to more effectively drive business forward.

This work is the basis for the road map. Management identifies the investments required to have the highest business impact with a commensurate level of effort (see figure 4-2). The road map provides a prioritized path forward. Based on the road map, the company can develop a high-level plan for initiatives that will align and optimize its activities, platforms, and resources with the previously identified goals.

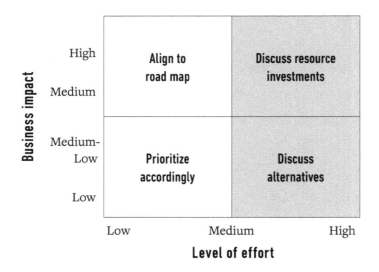

Figure 4-2. Matching level of effort to business impact.

GOVERNANCE AND MEASUREMENT ALIGN RESOURCES WITH VALUE

Once you've created the road map, a rigorous approach will allow you to tie the initiatives in the road map to results. This starts with defining the scope and methodology for each initiative. Next, you must create a governance structure to centrally manage the planning, guidance, inter-dependencies, and oversight of the initiatives, which can move forward using the organizational change management principles we described earlier in this chapter.

The rest of the path to success demands creating project teams for the initiatives, determining what benefits they promise to provide, and defining metrics to measure whether you're actually realizing those benefits.

This rigorous approach generates measurable improvements in outcomes:

- It identifies and prioritizes high-impact initiatives that are aligned with the maximum delivery of value.
- It enables fast decision-making and manages interdependencies among the change initiatives—generating early and visible successes.
- It maintains momentum and heads off risks from organizational resistance.
- It ensures that key contributors have the time to participate in the new initiative and addresses gaps in skills, tools, and methodologies.

At the center of this set of transformations is an established governance structure that empowers teams involved with tracking value, promoting change, and tracking risk, as shown in figure 4-3.

It's not enough to put this structure in place. The team must constantly measure whether the change is moving in the desired direction with the desired speed. This demands simple, transparent, scalable metrics that are aligned with where the value is coming from, balanced between financial and nonfinancial measures, built from a baseline all the key stakeholders agree on. Such metrics will include both measures of value, such as new products generated or units sold, and attitude metrics from employee surveys.

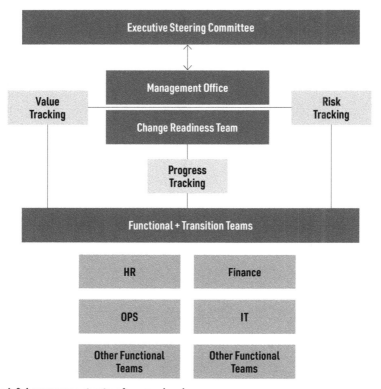

Figure 4-3. A governance structure for managing change.

To design these metrics, your organization must define the key performance drivers and indicators that could measure them, including a baseline for where things were before the initiative began. Confirm with stakeholders how the metrics align with goals and adjust them based on feedback about gaps or overlaps. Regularly report progress on these metrics.

A dashboard accessible to everyone involved in the initiatives can be a great help here. To build such a dashboard, consider your audience: Who needs to know which metrics and at what level of detail? Choose a design that will allow users to review the metrics on a single screen, highlighting three to five key values, charts, or tables with adequate context. Use consistent scales on charts and colors; avoid more than three or four digits of precision. Figure 4-4 shows an example of a dashboard for a systems launch.

Figure 4-4. Sample dashboard for a systems launch.

A FOCUS ON DATA AND ANALYTICS FUELS BETTER DECISIONS

Operational excellence depends on an accurate picture of what is happening in the business at any given moment. That picture depends on data. For that data to be useful, companies must adopt discipline and rigor in managing the platform that consumes dynamic data, wrangling it into a useful form, integrating data from diverse sources, and presenting it in easy-to-understand formats.

The objective here is to empower decision-makers to rapidly spot trends and insights and use that information to react quickly and intelligently. A business set up to use data in this way can be efficient, responsive, and in some cases predictive, moving with agility to take advantage of changing conditions.

Among all barriers that prevent effective response to changing conditions, lack of access to data-based insights ranks second, according to the business decision-makers in the Forrester Consulting survey. (Only lack of coordination across departments is more of a problem.) Thirty-two percent of decision-makers cited the inability to manage and distribute customer insights to the stakeholders that need them as a significant barrier to responsiveness.

An intelligent and systematic approach to actionable data requires four components.

First is data wrangling: transforming raw data into a usable form. Data can be complex and ambiguous. A sophisticated approach to this massive amount of data requires discovery to determine the full landscape of data sources, data cleansing to fix flaws like duplication and missing information, enrichment from aggregating multiple data sources, and regular audits to maintain the dependability and integrity of data. Tools like SQL rules engines can help with this task.

Second is data integration. Enterprises can have dozens or hundreds of data sources; making intelligent decisions requires integrating these sources into a unified view. While data on its own can be useful, unlocking the full value of data insights requires combining data from multiple sources. This is how you can surface previously unknown insights and generate more predictive opportunities. This activity depends on building a central data repository to synthesize data from varied sources and automating workflows to keep data sources up to date with tools like Alteryx, Tableau Prep, and Power BI.

Third is data visualization. Human decision-makers can't act on a flood of numbers; they respond better to data stories told visually. This means creating custom dashboards like the one shown in the previous section. It also means customizing what's shown on those dashboards based on what a specific decision-maker needs, both with regular reporting and with ad-hoc analyses supporting specific decisions.

Underlying all of these initiatives is a fourth effort: the creation of a trusted and dependable data platform that aggregates and manages the data that's being wrangled, integrated, and visualized. The platform is built with a data and information architecture that includes standards and guidelines, models that connect the data structures to what's happening in the business, rigorous operations that manage and monitor data facilities and protect them from unauthorized access or corruption, and support from developers to maintain the entire platform.

Emerging AI technologies will depend on this solid platform because, as AI and data expert Seth Earley writes, "there is no AI without IA [information architecture]."[13] But with a solid platform and analytics tools in place, enterprises can leverage advanced tools like machine learning to rapidly surface actionable insights, along with predictive analytics to prepare for what's likely to happen next.

Diverse organizations have taken advantage of these sorts of data initiatives. For example, one nonprofit organization used them to implement a staged data pipeline and a robust data warehouse to enable its senior decision-makers to get an accurate picture of advances in disease treatment. In another situation, during the consolidation of three companies, the team optimized processes defining customer segments and rules by integrating and automating data analysis from diverse data systems. (See the sidebar for more on challenges in mergers and acquisitions.)

FOUR STAGES TO OPERATIONAL EXCELLENCE

All of these operational excellence initiatives—developing and implementing operational road maps, implementing governance and measurement, setting up data and analytics, assuring the success of mergers and acquisitions (and some we haven't mentioned, such as automating business processes)—follow a common pattern.

They require organizational change management to enable the required changes in mindset. Organizational change management is fundamentally aligned with the four-stage process we described in chapter 2: It begins with exposing where the value is, is planned with systems thinking, moves forward by empowering teams, and stays on track with embedded feedback loops.

THE MERGERS AND ACQUISITIONS PLAYBOOK

In this chapter, we've discussed best practices for creating an organization that can thrive on change. When it comes to change, one of the biggest challenges an organization can deal with is the task of preparing for and then executing a major merger or acquisition.

Face it: Most mergers fail. As Clayton Christensen and colleagues wrote in *Harvard Business Review*, "companies spend more than $2 trillion on acquisitions every year. Yet study after study puts the failure rate of mergers and acquisitions somewhere between 70% and 90%."[14] As Christensen and his colleagues observed, "companies too often pay the wrong price and integrate the acquisition in the wrong way."

Integrating businesses is a massive juggling act with enormous possible pitfalls. The managers involved in the merger or acquisition must maintain day-to-day operations, plan and conduct the integration of the businesses, and imagine and realize a future state in which the integrated entity actually pays off as planned. Strategically, this requires identifying leaders, ensuring executive alignment, rationalizing strategy, setting expectations, and developing a plan for the execution. Tactically, it means setting goals and objectives, developing and implementing governance, rationalizing processes and initiatives, identifying and managing interdependencies, eliminating redundancies, and managing internal resource competition. It's little wonder that such a complex project doesn't succeed without a disciplined plan.

To maximize the chance of success in any merger or acquisition, executives must find answers to key questions. Strategy and leadership questions include:

- **Who is leading the integration?** Do you have representation from both companies? Do you have adequate representation from all functional areas? Who is empowered to make decisions?
- **What is the integration strategy?** What are your guiding principles? Do you know what you need to do by day one and what you can defer?
- **What synergies will you pursue?** Have you established synergy targets? Are you measuring progress to achieve those targets?
- **What are your priorities?** Have you identified and prioritized any existing strategic initiatives, such as IT upgrades or new product launches, and eliminated those that are not required?
- **What is the governance for the integration?** How will you communicate integration status to executives and other stakeholders? How are you managing risks and challenges?

There are also operational questions, including these:

- **What changes will customers see?** What will change on day one, and what will change later on? How do your people identify themselves to customers and suppliers as part of the merged company? Where do brand value and positive consumer sentiment reside, and how can they be maximized as part of the process?

- **What is the impact on your target company's workforce and your own?** Will jobs be cut? Have you identified critical personnel, and do you have a strategy to retain them?
- **How will you communicate about the deal?** Do you know what employees are concerned about? Have you met with them? What will you tell them? Do they have a means to raise concerns or get questions answered? How will you be consistent in messaging to employees, customers, suppliers, the community, and regulators?
- **How will the deal affect contracts?** What change of control provisions exist with the acquired companies' contracts? What's your plan to address those contracts?

In our experience, it's best to make plans according to the three stages of integration: first value preservation, then value realization, and finally value creation.

In the value preservation stage, stabilize the businesses and plan for the integration

The first step is to stabilize both organizations' businesses to preserve their current value. Value can erode because key customers or employees become concerned and may decide to use the merger as a reason to leave. Even if employees stay, managers distracted by the merger can cause the combined business to suffer a loss of productivity and operational effectiveness, a lack of near-term business focus and execution, and poor or undisciplined decision-making.

To avoid these risks, develop a "Day 1" operating plan to stabilize the business and set the strategic, financial, and operational objectives for the integration. Begin planning early to implement the steps we describe in the organizational change management section of this chapter.

These efforts include setting up an integration management office, designating integration teams, and communicating with them regularly. Develop a strategy for communicating, not just at the start of the integration but throughout the process. As part of the planning, maintain a master work schedule for risk remediation, integration, and existing initiatives.

In the value realization phase, assure the success and the benefits of the merger

The due diligence associated with the merger promises benefits: both cost savings and synergies.

All mergers promise to achieve cost savings through consolidation of redundant activities, economies of scale and increased buying power, better leverage of assets and resources of the combined firm, and lower corporate overhead. This stage is where you design and integrate the people, process, and technology functions of the merging organizations. Implement these plans carefully but without delay, because there is always uncertainty associated with job changes and job losses due to integration.

This is also when you begin to realize the planned synergies between the organizations. This demands careful planning. Identify, quantify, and, most importantly, *prioritize* synergy opportunities. Monitor and measure the value that is associated with these synergies and make course corrections as needed.

Managing the integration process includes an array of different regular communications efforts. These include weekly check-ins with the integration management office, working with steering committees from different functions and divisions, preparing and distributing weekly summaries of progress on merger activities, and briefing board members. This is also when integration leaders use surveys and other instruments to measure staff progress on the changes to their work and their mindsets that determine the cultural success of the merger.

The value realization phase is also where the risk ramps up. Engage and empower the project teams to make the right decisions, prioritize and monitor risks, and ensure that appropriate leaders perform the required change management, organizational, cultural, and communication activities to keep the merger or acquisition on track and delivering value.

In the value creation phase, pursue transformation

The general advice about business transformations in chapters 6 through 10 of this book continue to apply here. But in the specific case of mergers and acquisitions, the value creation phase is where you can identify and realize incremental benefits from the merged enterprise.

Once the business integration from the previous phase is well underway, you can take the next step of moving the business to a new operating model that creates competitive differentiation, as we describe later in this chapter. This is where it is possible to take the synergies from the previous phase and turn them into new capabilities that the business could never have had access to before.

These four stages are also intimately connected with the other operational excellence initiatives:

- **Exposing value defines the priorities for change in all operational excellence.** Any change for operational excellence requires a clearly articulated and communicated explanation of how it will enhance value. Operating models and road maps can help to clarify where change is needed and how it can be tied to value. The exposure of value is central to changes in governance, since such an explanation helps everyone know why the changes are necessary and how they relate to the company's biggest objectives. And data and analytics initiatives exist, fundamentally, to enable decision-makers to gain the insights they need to consistently and responsively improve the path to value.

- **Embracing systems thinking is central to realizing operational excellence.** The operational road map is a way to visualize the systems that make up an enterprise. Governance changes are a systematic way to implement changes that roll up to an overall improvement in operations. And data and analysis tools enable individual decisions to be made with a whole-enterprise context in mind. Operational excellence is impossible without systems thinking, since real progress requires a holistic view of the enterprise.

- **Empowered teams fuel operational excellence.** Rigid, centralized management can never be truly responsive. But empowering teams is scary, since without an organizational context, these teams have the potential to make decisions that are locally beneficial but globally detrimental. The overarching operational road map, smart governance structures, and integrated data insights provide the guardrails and guidance that keep empowered teams contributing to the enterprise goal of operational excellence.

- **Feedback loops keep operational excellence on track.** None of the plans in an operational road map or components of a governance model can be executed without feedback loops for course corrections. And data and analytics discipline surfaces the knowledge needed to know what's working and what needs to be changed. The operations of a responsive enterprise demand regularly updated, robust, and clear data feeds to remain efficient and adaptive to changes, both internal and external.

Continued attention to these stages will lead to continued improvements in operational excellence—and an enterprise that responds efficiently and quickly to change. But to go even further, enterprises must master the ultimate responsive skill: enterprise agility. That's what we discuss in the next chapter.

Chapter 5

ENTERPRISE AGILITY AS A NEW MINDSET

In September 2021, "Albert" was the head of product management for a division of a large technology company we'll call TechCo. Albert had come to the realization that his division was inexorably falling behind its competitors, and he now recognized that the key to TechCo being able to keep up was to embrace agility in all the division's activities.

While that sounds simple, it was quite difficult to consider. For one thing, the division included many veteran engineers and developers with twenty or more years of experience who were used to doing software development using a more traditional method known as waterfall, in which design, implementation, and verification were separate processes. At the TechCo division, this meant that engineers would respond to a set of requirements and build to that design for six months. Then, for another six months, they would respond to bug reports and fix bugs in what they had created. It was a development method that had stood the test of time, but one that was optimized for hitting a fixed target that was well defined ahead of time.

Regrettably for TechCo, when this division aimed at such fixed targets, the results were often obsolete and noncompetitive by the time they were released.

A second obstacle was the sheer size of the division. It included sixty development groups in North America and another 100 overseas. Any change would require a large number of developers to change the way they did their work.

Finally, the division had tried to embrace Agile methodologies twice before. Both attempts had failed. Such a history of failure had rendered the staff jaded to attempts to transform the way they worked.

Despite these challenges, Albert knew that the difficult change was necessary. Certainly, the division would need to embrace the Agile software development methodology that had become popular throughout the engineering world. But that would be insufficient. The division would need to not just *do* Agile, but to *be* agile. A change in methodology alone would not suffice—only a complete change in mindset would enable the division to move fast enough to remain competitive.

Albert convinced his peers, managers, and subordinates to undertake the challenge, then hired us to help him implement a plan to get there. He set a goal: Enhance the team's growth mindset, increasing its ability to consistently iterate, rapidly scale, and continuously focus on predictable outcomes. And to ensure that this was not just another exercise in pretending, he identified five measurable outcomes:

1. Standardize planning and requirements to increase delivery predictability.
2. Improve data hygiene and adopt technology enhancements to improve metrics and tracking.
3. Eliminate waste and context switching to increase team efficiency.
4. Adopt a standard meeting cadence and enhance status reporting to empower teams.
5. Measure and improve the team's maturity on standard Agile metrics to enable future scale.

With this vision laid out, the journey began. Hundreds of staff went through Agile training workshops, learning to develop in short, continuous sprints directed at customer goals instead of rigid predefined requirements. Teams would work on a "backlog" of feature requests, always focusing on the features with the highest value for customers. And they changed the way they collaborated: they'd meet every day for fifteen minutes, but stop participating in wasteful nonrelevant meetings that were sapping their development time.

TechCo set up an Agile Center of Excellence with highly trained staff able to answer the development group's questions about the new methodology. Trained team members fanned out and, a few teams at a time, changed the way the division delivered to be far more responsive and customer-focused.

Teams started to have early success. One team moved quickly enough to deliver a feature that generated $40 million in sales. Multiple teams recaptured 30% or more of time that had been wasted in unproductive meetings, saving an estimated $12 million worth of developer time.

But after about one year of progress, despite early success among the teams, Albert's efforts at TechCo stalled. There are two key lessons from this story about change.

First, while development teams had begun to realize the gains from Agile methods, old and established patterns rose up to block additional progress. For one thing, the teams were still reporting progress using old waterfall metrics of success. Among those measures were lines of code created—a metric that had little to do with actual value created for customers. When success metrics are still rooted in the past, the value of Agile methods becomes harder to justify.

And second, the work or results do not always speak for themselves. Albert was unable to establish strong executive support for the program, and his budget to continue this work needed to be approved by someone higher up the chain. The program's results and the impact must be communicated across functional areas of the business and up the leadership chain. This clearly positions the work as indispensable so when budget cuts come—and eventually they always do—change projects or pilots will not be considered for reduction or cutting because they are saving the company money and enabling efficiency.

Despite the meaningful impact on efficiency, effectiveness, and financial performance at TechCo, there was a limited tolerance for failure and recovery. Failure and quick learning are at the heart of Agile methods. Without the ability to fail and recover, Albert's division could not embrace agility. But given the division's previously fading performance, few in management had much tolerance for failure.

In the end, the TechCo division was attempting to do two things at once: Embrace a new Agile way of working that could respond to customer needs quickly and satisfy previous measures and metrics of what it meant to be productive. No one can possibly succeed serving two masters.

While the end of this story has yet to be written, without a continued commitment to a responsive way of working, the old ways of doing development are likely to reemerge.

ENTERPRISE AGILITY PROMISES FAR MORE THAN AGILE APPLICATION DEVELOPMENT

The Agile movement has swept through the world of software development. More than half the companies in a recent Forrester global survey had adopted Agile development practices.[15] Agile development methods like sprints, scrum, minimum viable products, and feature backlogs are now common among development teams. If you just want a book on Agile software methods, there are hundreds on Amazon. (See sidebar.)

As the changes at TechCo showed, compared with traditional development methods, Agile development is faster, more efficient, and more responsive to customer needs. But in most organizations, agile thinking stops once you move outside the software and development teams.

AGILE METHODS

Agile is a development philosophy in which cross-functional teams identify and make improvements in software based on a continually evolving set of requirements. It is adaptive—that is, those continual improvements are based on observed changes and needs—as opposed to a predictive software development model like waterfall in which the requirements are set in advance of development.

The philosophy of Agile is based around contributors collaborating, getting things working quickly, meeting the needs of customers, and responding to change. But modern Agile methods are distinguished by several distinctive practices. These include:

- "Sprints" of one to four weeks during which developers identify and work on a set of requirements to deliver an iterative improvement in the software.
- Teams that cross functions, with representation from people who plan, analyze, design, code, and test the software.
- Brief, face-to-face, daily "standup" meetings to resolve issues and answer questions, with a corresponding reduction in other wasteful meetings.
- A product owner or product manager who represents the customer and the customer's needs.

There are various well-established flavors of Agile software development. For example, in scrum, there is a scrum master whose job is to coach the team and clear any impediments to their success, the list of features worked on in any iteration is drawn from a prioritized list of desired items known as a backlog, and a "burndown chart" shows the remaining work to be done at any point within the sprint. In Kanban, the work operates off a visual display that shows work in progress, and desired features are described in terms of user stories.

According to Digital.ai's "2022 State of Agile Report," 52% of Agile developers adopted Agile to accelerate time to market, and 26% were adopting Agile practices as an element of a company-wide digital transformation. More than seven in ten developers were satisfied with their companies' Agile practices.

Even the Agile developers recognize the challenge. According to Digital.ai's 2022 survey of Agile developers, approximately 40% report a lack of leadership participation, a lack of knowledge about Agile, organizational resistance to change, and inadequate management support as barriers to the adoption of Agile throughout the organization.[16]

To be sure, the boundary between technology and business is increasingly tenuous because technology is woven into every business process. Sales, marketing, product development, finance, human resources, and operations: Can a company in the 2020s do any of these functions without technology products, systems, processes, and databases? If the technology improves at the speed of Agile but the functions continue to operate in a slow and traditional way, the organization cannot be responsive to change.

Given the rate of change organizations are now dealing with, you have to ask, "Couldn't we achieve improvements in other functional areas of our business by applying those same Agile methods?" Rick Schantz, our

VP of enterprise agility, explains the reasoning beyond enterprise agility this way: Agile thinking and process must be a value embraced by every function, department, team, and process within the enterprise.

What is enterprise agility? It is a way of working across the enterprise that emphasizes speed, consistent direction, and responsive course corrections over rigid, long-term planning. An agile enterprise is capable of adjusting in real time to meet whatever priorities arise, always improving to deliver maximum value. That mindset pervades every department and function at every level of the company, from line workers to senior managers. Each function constantly improves its responsiveness to its customers, whether those customers are the actual customers of the business or other employees.

There are major benefits to introducing Agile methodologies across an enterprise, adopting an agile mindset, and scaling the agile approach. Benefits such as a 30% increase in efficiency, a ten-times increase in decision-making speed, a 30% increase in customer satisfaction, or a thirty-point improvement in employee engagement are all possible.

The whole organization moves with a unified, responsive purpose. Business strategy and execution are aligned. Everything moves faster, and business results improve with a high degree of predictability and quality.

But while these gains are tantalizing, recognize that this is a profound transformation that requires constant perseverance—the perseverance that Albert's division at TechCo lacked. Executive priorities and budgets are typically built for a world without rapid change. The deliverable for the enterprise is no longer fixed: The deliverable is improvements in serving customers and the business benefits that accrue from that. As a result, priorities and budgets may shift from month to month. There is always progress, but not along a predictable path. For leaders accustomed to control, living with that uncertainty is a major mind shift.

Doing Agile is common in any organization that includes software development. But *being* agile is not. The transformation to being an agile enterprise is where the real payoff lies.

DO COMPANIES HAVE WHAT IT TAKES TO RESPOND TO CHANGING CUSTOMER NEEDS?

Companies *say* they want to respond to customers. In the Forrester Consulting survey of business decision-makers, the most popular items in the top three corporate priorities were meeting customer demand and expectations; understanding customers' changing needs and preferences; accelerating response to shifts in customer and market needs; and implementing organizational changes to better align with evolving customer, product, and service strategies.

Decision-makers also believe that enterprise agility is important. In our survey, 78% said that adjusting their organizations and operations to accommodate changes in the business environment was either important or mission-critical.

But in the same survey, one in three cited problems with lack of coordination across teams, and similar numbers complained of the inability to manage and distribute customer insights to teams. More than one in four complained of lack of senior executive support for becoming a responsive enterprise (see figure 5-1).

The will is there. Companies just don't know how to act on it.

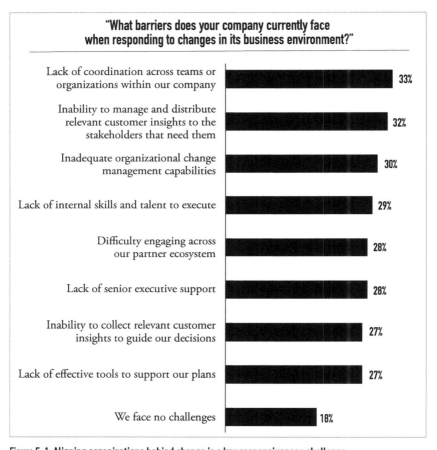

Figure 5-1. Aligning organizations behind change is a key responsiveness challenge.
Source: A commissioned study conducted by Forrester Consulting on behalf of Celerity, November 2021. Base: 418 North American digital strategy decision-makers.

THE ELEMENTS OF ENTERPRISE AGILITY

Let's get specific. What is it like to be an agile enterprise? Recognizing the rapidity of change in business environments, three-year plans, and even one-year plans, are out the window. Instead, managers set the vision about where the organization will go, and the functions make adjustments to address that vision. The enterprise aligns strategy with execution, so each move that any part of the enterprise makes becomes a step toward that overall vision.

Part of that speed is for teams and workers to think about one thing at a time, rather than switching contexts all the time. While we are advocates of systems thinking (see chapter 7), in an agile enterprise each improvement comes from a team concentrating on and improving one modular piece at a time.

For that mindset to change, every group must accept this set of principles.

- Make satisfying your customer the first and foremost priority.
- Embrace the need for and value of ongoing change.
- Deliver improvements frequently (early and often).
- Prioritize action and experimentation over planning and output.
- Accept that FAIL is your "First Attempt In Learning" that leads to innovation.
- Reduce risks with progress in small iterative steps.
- Measure progress against value and outcomes, not raw output or activity metrics.

- Celebrate every success, every failure, and every instance of waste eliminated.
- Recognize that engaging your employees is the foundation for all other success.

AGILE BEYOND IT

You may wonder what this even looks like outside of the development of a software product. But with the right perspective, you can see how it applies to every element of the organization.

Consider a marketing program. That program might include a website with landing pages, advertising, lead capture, public relations, email marketing, social media, and so on. Perhaps the marketers are tasked with marketing a new product that's coming out in February.

In an agile enterprise, the marketers embrace a philosophy of agile responsiveness to changing conditions. There may be a planned set of tactics for marketing the product, but that plan is not rigidly fixed. If a competitor gains visibility, the marketing team may shift its focus, quickly launching a new email campaign, optimizing for different keywords, or scrambling to begin PR outreach. If the product launch is delayed, the focus of the marketing campaign may shift from selling to capturing leads for future use. If the organization has a need for immediate revenue, the campaign may shift again, discounting prices and prioritizing conversions. Rather than becoming frustrated by the changes in their carefully constructed plans, the marketers take pride in their ability to tap into their skills to address whatever is happening at any given moment.

Or consider a human resources department tasked with recruiting. There may be an established process for screening resumes and setting up interviews. But in an agile enterprise, that process is not set in stone. If an industry-wide layoff generates thousands of newly unemployed prospects, the recruiting group could pivot to outreach based on changes in people's LinkedIn profiles or ramp up its messaging to existing employees to boost referrals. Or if the organization's needs for new hires rapidly ramp up, the recruiting group could retool its interview processes to work faster and more effectively. HR isn't often known as a responsive part of the enterprise, but in an agile enterprise it needs to change how it behaves, just as any other department would.

Agile methods in one part of the business, like technology, generate some gains. But agile methods in *all* parts of the business are what creates responsiveness. There are no rigid roadblocks—everything can move in the direction that conditions dictate, constantly becoming better at serving customers.

A PRODUCT MINDSET

Not everything that an enterprise does is a product. Agile methods are most effective for product development. So how can agile methods apply to the nonproduct parts of an organization?

These parts must adopt a product mindset. Consider the qualities products have:

- They are designed for customers.

- They succeed if they deliver value to those customers.

- They have a set of features.

- It's possible to improve those features.

- Multidisciplinary teams create them (design, development, manufacturing, operations, quality control, etc.).

- There is a product manager whose job is to maximize the value of the product.

Look closely at that list. *None of those qualities are exclusive to products.* In other words, you can apply a product mindset to anything an organization does.

Gartner defines a product as "a named collection of business capabilities valuable to a defined customer segment" (where customers can be external or internal).[17] A product may comprise any combination of software, hardware, facilities, and services required to deliver the entire experience. And that includes functions that we don't typically think of as products.

When companies adopt a product mindset, they shift from a functional focus on projects and systems to a strategic and collaborative focus on capabilities, products, and value received from stakeholders (see table 5-1). And they empower employees to proactively identify problems to be solved, adapt to the changing needs of the end user, and deliver collaborative, coordinated, and iterative solutions.

PRODUCTS	PROJECTS
Implemented by stable, predictable value streams	Implemented by temporary teams that disband after work is completed
Scope is variable	Scope is fixed and must be implemented
Progress is measured as outcomes against the hypothesized benefit	Progress is measured based on a work breakdown structure and task completion
Lean-product business case, based on benefit hypotheses	Detailed business case based on speculative ROI
Implementation follows build-measure-iterate cycle	Implementation typically follows a phase-gated, sequential process
Commitment is evaluated on delivery of a minimum viable product	Up-front commitment is made to the entire project scope

Table 5-1. Comparison of product mindset to project mindset.

What does this product mindset look like? Take customer service as an example. Like a product, it delivers value to customers. The team's tasks include hiring and training customer service representatives, methods for how those reps deliver service, tools and technologies that the reps use in their work, methods that the team uses to measure its success, and so on. You can measure the success of that delivery and improve it by improving the hiring and training methods, the customer service systems, the scripts, the service delivery channels, and so on. So why can't customer service be treated like a product with a product manager and a value of continuous improvement?

If you're in the finance department reporting financial results, your customers may be managers within the company, but you're still creating a product—that is, a set of financial reports that others depend on.

Adopting a product mindset allows any department or function to access the benefits of Agile methods: A focus on customer needs. Prioritizing improvements based on those needs. A product manager. A frequent cadence of short meetings along with the elimination of wasteful meetings. A vision that everyone is working toward. The ability to pivot quickly. Alignment of strategy and execution.

Simply put, a product mindset allows any team to make decisions that will frequently and continuously improve its contributions to the business. And if every department is doing that, the whole enterprise becomes agile and responsive.

COMBINING LEAN AND AGILE MINDSETS

Agile is about responsiveness. Lean, the management philosophy pioneered by Toyota in the twentieth century, focuses on efficiency. The two are not only compatible, they are mutually reinforcing and more effective together.

The core of Lean is the quest to eliminate waste. Waste, simply understood, is any process or component that does not contribute to customer value.

The Lean methodology focuses on five key principles:

1. **Value.** Identify what the customer finds valuable in a product.

2. **Value stream.** Map each step in conceiving and delivering the product, and identify how it contributes—or fails to contribute—to value.

3. **Flow.** Ensure all processes that create value work together as efficiently as possible, with no delays or disruptions.

4. **Pull.** Limit inventory of "work in progress" by creating a system where elements are delivered as soon as they are needed, but no sooner.

5. **Seek perfection.** Continually find new ways to improve efficiency and eliminate waste.

A team operating on Agile principles can make constant improvements, not just in products, but in how they are delivered. So a Lean Agile mindset is one that seeks not just maximum value for customers, but also minimum waste in delivering that value.

Lean prompts team members to question potentially wasteful action. Why are we doing this activity? Could we eliminate it and spend our energy on things that actually matter? This is part of the process of constant innovation, testing, and improvement that powers an agile enterprise.

STEPS IN THE ENTERPRISE AGILITY TRANSFORMATION

Every agile or product transformation needs a leader. This might be the chief experience officer or the chief operating officer, but it must be someone with influence across the organization who can advocate for change. Because unless the shift to agility is coordinated, its benefits will be attenuated.

The process of that transformation then follows the four transformation steps we introduced in chapter 2: exposing value, embracing systems thinking, empowering teams, and embedding feedback loops.

Expose the value and goals for the agile enterprise at the start

Why is the organization undertaking this transformation? Possible reasons include increasing speed, reacting more quickly to market forces, eliminating waste, or improving customer satisfaction and retention. All of those are closely connected to the value that the enterprise creates.

It's crucial to identify the goals up front, because without those goals, there is no good reason for the leaders, managers, and staff to buy into the process. For example, at TechCo, the main goals were to increase the speed of development and eliminate waste.

Once that value is established, leaders need to encourage everyone to embrace the vision for it. There must be a realistic, shared road map outlining how the organization will train staff in Agile methods and mindsets, along with outlining how the first teams will implement Agile in their work. Leaders must share regular messages and updates and invest in training staff in the Agile method of doing things. The objective should be to get everyone on board and aligned with the Agile vision.

To succeed, this training must work from both top down and bottom up. The training for senior leaders should emphasize the organization's goals and the value in the transformation, the language used to communicate it, and the metrics used to measure and deliver business benefits. Crucially, the training must help leaders embrace a management philosophy based on *outcomes*, such as improvements in customer satisfaction, rather than *output*, such as lines of code written or releases completed.

A different set of training is necessary to help the rank-and-file contributors to embrace Agile methodology in the work of their teams. This more practical training should start with training cross-functional staff in a small number of teams that will actually pilot the methods.

Leaders should also establish an Agile Center of Excellence. This is a dedicated cross-functional set of coaching resources staffed with experts who've succeeded with Agile methods in the past. In addition to its coaching role, this team provides the information necessary to communicate ongoing successes to the organization.

Embrace systems thinking for Agile by managing portfolios and antipatterns

Agile cannot succeed if it is embedded in an organization that maintains old, traditional, nonresponsive ways of working, focused on deliberate, carefully designed plans and compensated solely on outputs. Even so, the first sparks of agility in a company must necessarily begin against a backdrop of traditional thinking.

So organizations must carefully plan the transformation. To start, the organization needs to examine its portfolio of activities and determine where Agile methods can best generate early success.

It's also important to recognize and counteract "antipatterns." An antipattern is a commonly used process within an organization that purports to solve a problem but generates its own inertia. For example, at TechCo, the waterfall metrics used to measure and reward developer progress functioned as an antipattern.

Managing the Agile portfolio and heading off antipatterns are good examples of how systems thinking can improve the chances that a nascent transformation like enterprise agility can take hold, spread, and succeed.

One more high-level insight is necessary here. Executives want a clear connection between budget allocation and result. They want to know how much something is going to cost, how long it is going to take, and what will be the outcome. Agile starts with a desired outcome, but it can be challenging to identify a fixed schedule or rigid cost structure. This is a monumental departure from traditional ways of making business decisions and doing business. As a result, executive-level buy-in is crucial to the success of enterprise agility.

Empowered teams are central to getting enterprise agility started

Once you've selected teams to launch and trained their staff, you're ready to light the spark that will generate early successes. First, identify a small number of teams that are well-prepared to prioritize value and embrace incremental delivery. Ensure that each of these teams has representation from all key functions and individuals in key roles like product manager. Set a clear direction for the team based on metrics like value for customers and efficiency. And have one member of the team regularly check back with the experts (potentially in an Agile Center of Excellence) to keep the team on track and answer questions.

As teams succeed, the organization must socialize and spread that success. Continue to train staff and cycle them through teams to boost the agile mindset and practices. And manage the portfolio of Agile teams in such a way that each new team reinforces the others, contributes to broader goals, and makes progress against the metrics you have established.

Embedded feedback loops are essential to the agile transformation

Everyone involved in an agile transformation has moments in which they wonder, "Why are we doing this?" This especially applies to leaders, who are giving up the appearance of control in exchange for promised gains.

At the team level, feedback is vital to every Agile sprint. When a team member implements a change, the next logical step is to see if it was an actual improvement: if it improved metrics like time spent on the site or reduced customer complaints. Longer-term, teams will also be measuring metrics like revenue or customer satisfaction. We go into more detail on this in chapter 9 when we discuss feedback loops.

But even as teams are making gains on their own products, leaders need to monitor the gains that the whole enterprise is making. This is a function of the Center of Excellence, and a key indicator for the overall agile transformation leader to track.

There are of course top-line metrics such as revenue, customer retention, growth, and cost savings. But Agile methods also allow measurement of more detailed metrics such as these:

- Customer experience scores (from customer surveys)
- Data hygiene/data quality
- Cycle time (reduction in feature cycle time and production delays)
- Defects (reducing number, frequency, severity of defects)
- Defect resolution (reduction in cycle time)
- Feature production accuracy (accuracy in predictions of features or release dates)
- Feature value accuracy (improved prioritization of feature backlogs)
- Average cost of production (improved feature-to-staff ratio)

With this number of possible metrics, each enterprise and its leaders must go back to the value analysis and the vision to make choices on what to prioritize. Is customer experience more important than feature accuracy? The preferred metrics will provide management with feedback on what's working, what's lagging, and what changes will better boost the preferred measures. This allows the enterprise as a whole to behave with more agility, even as the individual teams are pursuing Agile methods for their individual products and processes.

IDENTIFYING AND SURMOUNTING OBSTACLES

As the TechCo experience showed, there are plenty of things that can derail or halt an agile enterprise transformation.

The most common is just a failure to identify and quantify metrics to prove that progress is taking place. If you plan ways to measure improvements as you go along, when the time comes to approve continued budget or to fend off a challenge from those who still want to do things the old way, you will have no proof that you are succeeding in a way that matters to the business. And that's a sure prescription for the transformation to stall—and it's exactly what happened in the division at TechCo.

It's also common for senior managers to get cold feet when they realize that they're no longer in charge of every detailed change that happens and that they cannot easily measure what each team member is doing at any given moment.

Leaders need to become comfortable with ambiguity—with improvements in metrics like speed and customer experience rather than success on milestones fixed months or years earlier that have become irrelevant and out of date.

Another source of failed transformation is attempting to deliver on both old and new ways of working at the same time. A team that is committed to the Agile methodologies must work in an agile way—and get rewarded based on agile success. If that team is still rewarded based on old-style output metrics, it's tough to stay the course with Agile methodologies. Among Agile developers surveyed by Digital.ai, 42% said they were still dealing with legacy systems based on old reporting methods. Maintaining old compensation and bonus plans is a sure path to undermining any agility transformation.

Perhaps the most pernicious problem is making progress on process improvements, but failing to change the overall corporate mindset. If all the software teams are using Agile methods but the enterprise itself is not behaving with agility, the change will increasingly focus on technology only. A transformation that proceeds by half-measures cannot realize its full potential.

THE PROMISE OF THE RESPONSIVE ENTERPRISE

Massive gains are possible. At first, companies and leaders buy into Agile methodology concepts. They begin practicing agility in their work. And then, if the effort doesn't stall out, they begin to change the culture.

It becomes less of an effort to think about agility and more of a habit. Challenges become opportunities. People respond to change quickly.

Add this mindset to customer centricity and operational excellence and the result is a responsive enterprise—one that has a sustainable competitive advantage.

Part III

STAGES IN THE RESPONSIVE ENTERPRISE TRANSFORMATION

Chapter 6

EXPOSE THE VALUE OF THE TRANSFORMATION

Senior IT executive JT Scott has been instrumental in multiple corporate transformation efforts at large companies. He'll be the first to tell you that it's not easy.

"Most of these transformations fail due to institutional inertia," he points out. "The biggest issue is that corporations have an antibody that resists changes." The old ways of doing things are familiar, and when employees are uncertain, they fall back on habit. That pushback can doom a transformation effort.

If you're going to attempt a transformation, the challenge of inertia makes two things imperative.

"The first thing I look at is, what goal are they trying to achieve? What's driving the need to innovate or to change?" asks Scott. "Because it's not worth undertaking an initiative this broad unless you have a clearly defined goal that *delivers value to the business*. Transformations happen because something fundamentally isn't working or could be working much better. That could be ebbing critical progress or delays in responding to clear needs—but if it's trending in the wrong direction, there comes a time to act."

Second, you must clearly communicate that value, repeatedly, from the top down, from the bottom up, across all management levels, and in every modality possible. "You have to do all aspects of communication," Scott says. "Verbal: have a meeting where they can hear you. Written: so that it is documented why you're doing this. Collaborative sessions, with time for feedback. Listen to the employees. And implement training sessions." Communication at the start—and throughout the transformation—is imperative.

Look back at the examples we've described so far in this book, and you'll see that each transformation effort began with a clear analysis and communication of the value to the business.

The large bank, FinCo, in chapter 1 recognized an urgent need for more agility in the face of rapid change in financial services.

ClinicCo, the clinic operator in chapter 2, was facing productivity and resource challenges that only an overhaul in scheduling could fix.

To energize growth and retain customers, CredCo, the credit union in chapter 3, needed a renewed focus on customer centricity and a different way of innovating.

Also in chapter 3, HealthCo, the health care company that improved the onboarding process in its cancer centers recognized that one of its main sources of value was attracting and connecting with patients early in the process.

RetailCo, the large retailer in chapter 4, couldn't enable faster value-laden decisions without a significantly more responsive focus on serving its internal customers.

And TechCo, the technology company in chapter 5, desperately needed to embrace agility to deal with the rapid pace of change in its industry.

All of these needs were fundamental and urgent. All were motivated by an essential need to be more responsive to change. And all required not just a clear focus on the value they would create, but an ability to articulate that value in ways that their employees could latch onto and embrace to get them through the change.

"Your organization risks everything, from low job satisfaction to higher turnover to instability," says Scott. "People in a transformation start to wonder, can I even do it the new way? The longer you draw out that change, the more uncertainty people have."

As Scott wisely points out, "There is also a need for psychological safety." Workers are anxious enough already: 41% of millennials and 46% of Gen Zs say they feel stressed all or most of the time.[18] Anxiety is not just unhealthy for workers; it's also a destroyer of productivity and teamwork. To successfully create transformational change, it's imperative to expose the value of what everyone is going to go through; you must clearly articulate why the change is worth it. Only then will the process of transforming succeed.

EVEN WHEN IT'S DESPERATELY NEEDED, TRANSFORMING IS DIFFICULT

It's always easiest to keep doing things the way you've always done them. That is, of course, until that approach is clearly leading the enterprise in the wrong direction.

At such a moment, leaders consider the major step of transforming a department or enterprise. A transformation can include a change in strategy—for example, targeting a new set of customers or emphasizing a new class of products—but it goes further than that. It's a change in the way the organization does business. A transformation often encompasses changes in how the business is organized, how work is done, how leaders measure success, and how the people working there must grow. That's a much more far-reaching shift than just tweaking strategy. And leaders must recognize that a transformation is never "done."

These sorts of major shifts can only happen when the need is stark and unmistakable. As a result, they often happen in the midst of stressful times for the organization. There is pressure for profit from the highest levels. Teams are overwhelmed with work. Middle managers struggle with keeping their teams productive while aligning their goals with the business. And often, in such situations, competitors are circling, sometimes with a disruptive model that's very hard for a rigid organization to compete with by just chugging ahead in the same direction. Regardless of the cause, it is the leaders' responsibility to clearly communicate why change is required and why individuals in the organization should adopt new habits.

Corporate transformations promise to make organizations more responsive to change. But because they are so profound, they don't always succeed.

A study by Boston Consulting Group, published in 2018 in *MIT Sloan Management Review*, analyzed US public companies with a market cap of at least $10 billion between 2004 and 2016.[19] According to the study:

> At any given point in the 12-year period we studied, 32% of all large companies were experiencing a severe deterioration in TSR [total shareholder return], and that share has stayed roughly constant in recent years. We also found that successful recovery from a severe episode of deterioration is the exception rather than the norm: Only one quarter of the companies were able to outperform their industry in the short and long run after the point of deterioration. Moreover, transformations appear to be getting somewhat riskier over time, as the rate of success fell from approximately 30% in 2001 to 25% by 2012. This pattern of frequent failure in turnarounds is striking.

A similar analysis by three professional services organizations analyzed 128 large global companies involved in transformation efforts between 2016 and 2020. That study, published in *Harvard Business*

Review, found that only 22% of companies pursuing transformation were successful.[20]

TRANSFORMATIONAL SUCCESS BEGINS WITH AN ANALYSIS OF VALUE

With these stark statistics in mind, leaders must take deliberate steps to ensure the success of any transformational effort. That starts with rigorous analysis to expose the value of the change, and it continues with effective communication and training to embed that value in the minds of the workforce. Speed is important, but it is equally important to clarify the direction that the organization is going and the destination it is aiming for. In physics, velocity equals speed plus direction. Similarly, a corporation's transformation needs not just speed but also movement in a coordinated, effective direction.

So what does it take to analyze the value of a transformation?

Start with "the burning platform." The analogy is to an oil rig fire: Nobody wants to jump until it becomes clear that staying on the rig is more dangerous than leaping. Similarly, a transformation generally begins with urgent motivating factors. Those factors typically boil down to one of three possibilities:

1. **Pains.** Identify challenges interfering with the organization's ability to accomplish its goals.
2. **Gains.** Specify new opportunities that would be in reach after the transformation.

3. **Productivity and growth.** Create a transformed organization that is more vibrant, efficient, and profitable.

Once the motivating factors are clear, leaders must get down to specifics. Transforming won't succeed if the value is vague and the proposed change is ill-defined. That means leaders must create concrete answers to these questions:

- **What is the value you expect to gain?** This needs to be a statement that leaders and workers in the organization can embrace. For example, "We will be able to address changes in customer needs more quickly" or "We will align investments in technology with the most pressing needs of the business." This statement of value is most effective with a clear and direct connection to financial metrics like profit and growth.

- **Who are the stakeholders that will receive the value?** In any transformation, the key stakeholders—leaders, managers, employees, and other parts of the business—will inevitably ask the question, "What's in it for me?" For leaders, the transformation needs to promise a sustained and measurable improvement in some element of how their business runs, such as speed to market or market-share growth. Employees want to know how the new way of working will enable them to contribute to the business and succeed personally. Managers need to understand how to translate the promised gains for the organization into terms that the workers can understand. And other parts of the business not directly in the path of the transformation will want to know how their own results and work will improve as a result of the transformation.

- **How will the change deliver the value?** The answer to this question is a plan: a road map for what will change and how, including messaging to stakeholders and training or upskilling programs if necessary.

- **How will you measure the result?** The delivery road map needs to be tied to concrete metrics like adoption levels, employee attitudes, and productivity increases. There should be a plan not just to identify these metrics, but also to create specific methods to measure them and to publicize the results.

- **When will the organization recognize the value?** Time frame matters. Transformation needs to start quickly, but typically won't near success for twelve to twenty-four months. While a transformation is never fully "done," all plans need milestones along the way where the leaders can verify progress. A change that won't pay off for three to five years is much harder to justify; stakeholders are more likely to tire of the effort, and market conditions may shift so much that the results are no longer as relevant.

EXPOSING THE CASE FOR VALUE TAKES A DELIBERATE PLAN

Defining the value of transforming is essential, but is only the first step. What happens next is messaging, training, and socializing the message.

Speed is essential here: Your plan must be designed to move quickly. In an interview with McKinsey & Company, Davor Tomašković, who led transformation efforts in three different industries, points out that "it is particularly critical to move fast and demonstrate early success when workforce morale and management credibility are low."[21] JT Scott, a veteran of multiple transformation efforts, agrees. "The bigger the team, the faster you have to go. Or else you risk getting caught living in two worlds," he adds. There's nothing deadlier than a half-completed transformation with some employees pulling forward and others sliding backward.

The transformation starts with a clear story for senior managers and by extension, the teams they lead. Articulate the message not just with verbal messages but in writing, so people can refer back to it, as well as in in-person training sessions. All the messages must be unified and consistent so there is no mistaking what's planned. During JT Scott's transformation experiences, he put constant effort into listening to staff, understanding their concerns, and addressing them. The focus is explaining what the transformation means for the company and the individual departments, but a lot of the listening is about "What does this mean for me, for my job, and for my job security?"

And don't stop at communicating with the affected departments and people. Transformations in one function or geography often have profound effects on business partners in other groups. Communication of the value of the transformation needs to encompass leaders and managers in those groups as well. "You must make sure those business partners are aligned," says Scott, "and that they see the vision and can support it."

It's also useful to take this opportunity to train employees in the skills they'll need to master in the new organization, whether that's a product approach, design thinking, customer experience, change management, an agile mindset, or anything else. Upskilling staff communicates that their contributions remain essential to the organization. A 2023 Randstad Workmonitor survey found that 25% of workers want to be retrained for new roles.[22] And another 2023 Randstad study found 76% of HR execs are placing a greater emphasis on skills development and career engagement.[23]

Stamina is key, because there is always resistance: People will point out that similar challenges were tried and failed in the past. And you must be compassionate along the way, because the disruptions associated with change are real. As we described with the major retailer in chapter 4, pilot the change with some groups, learn, and quickly extend those lessons to the rest of the organization.

Communicating value is the foundational first step in any transformation. After that, you need to develop a clear understanding of how the transformation will impact the organization as a whole. And that demands systems thinking, as we'll describe in the next chapter.

Chapter 7

EMBRACE AN OVERARCHING PHILOSOPHY OF SYSTEMS THINKING

Anyone can improve *part* of a business, but if you make one group's job easier by making other groups' jobs harder, have you really made an improvement?

The challenge is to visualize enterprises as systems. Every change you create generates ripples throughout the system. This means that to be effective with a transformation, you must employ systems thinking; that is, to develop a holistic understanding of how parts of the business are connected. Embrace this philosophy, and you can create change that makes an overall improvement, not just a tweak limited to one local process or phenomenon.

Consider the case studies in the chapters that preceded this one and how they reflect a systems perspective.

At FinCo, the bank in chapter 1, the pandemic response needed to cut across everything the bank did, from branch operations to government pandemic loans. This broad response would have an impact on the bank's websites, its online banking tools, its loan origination and processing activities, and its customer service operations. The solution wasn't just to put up a new website for pandemic purposes—it was to make sure that the content was properly conceived as a single source of answers for customers, thus benefitting all the affected parts of the bank.

At ClinicCo, the dialysis clinic chain in chapter 2, the improvements in its scheduling tool are an excellent example of systems thinking. ClinicCo's problems included moving personnel around, communicating with those personnel, employing safety and regulatory compliance, addressing patient needs, allocating equipment and suppliers, and countless other processes. Scheduling served as a hub for the clinic's operations. So the improvements in the scheduling tool were effective because they appropriately encompassed an impact on the whole organization.

At CredCo, the credit union in chapter 3, the innovations in dispute resolution needed to appropriately address customer needs, customer service operations, and back-end data pulls. At RetailCo, the store chain in chapter 4, the company remade financial systems development efforts in a way that touched processes from inventory management to merchandising to financial reporting. And at TechCo in chapter 5, the shift to an agile mindset required a transformation in the way the designers, hardware and software developers, and testers did their work.

When these improvements succeeded, they do so because they treated the enterprise within which they were deployed as a *system*. Almost all successful change efforts require an enterprise-wide set of improvements that can only succeed when leaders take a systems perspective on the whole enterprise to identify improvements that apply broadly, rather than just advantaging one department or group over another.

WHY USE SYSTEMS THINKING?

In a word, systems thinking is about impact. It ensures that a planned transformation can be designed for maximum effectiveness and sustained change.

There are two key reasons for this.

First, thinking that encompasses the sum of the parts is more powerful than proposing point solutions. You can't move a whole organization forward by just exerting effort in one spot. And in most cases, you cannot succeed with efforts in one location without support from the broader organization. You must move all the pieces forward at once.

And second, taken together, the people, processes, and technology involved in an organization roll up to create the *culture* at an organization. Culture is the mindset (or mental models) formed from the intersection of people, processes, and technologies (underlying structures) that result in an individual's daily behaviors and habits (events and patterns). The mindset change that is central to large-scale organizational transformations is shown on the surface through behaviors and habits. You cannot make change happen without acknowledging and addressing that culture and how it might need to change.

Part of systems thinking is the recognition of the antipatterns we mentioned in the previous chapter: established behaviors that resist change. Anyone who has attempted to make a change in any part of an organization knows that inertia is powerful—the system pushes back. Recognizing and addressing antipatterns becomes integral to any potential solution to the problem.

Systems thinking expands the potential choices for solving difficult problems. It generates more options for clearly articulating a solution. If you're trying to solve an ongoing challenge, rather than a one-off problem, systems thinking is absolutely necessary.

ROOT CAUSE ANALYSIS, INCLUDING JOURNEY MAPPING AND THE FIVE WHYS

The question "Why is there a problem here?" is surprisingly difficult to answer. It demands a look at the root causes of organizational issues, causes that remain hidden without a rigorous systems view of how an organization functions.

The customer experience process of journey mapping or service blueprinting that we mentioned in chapter 3 is a good example of systems thinking. In service blueprints, a team looks at the process a customer experiences, for example, processing a change of address for cable television service. The team starts by looking at the steps in the customer experience (for example, examining a bill to figure out how to contact the cable company, calling customer service, setting a date for the move, moving to a new location, returning old equipment, getting new equipment, connecting devices, and so on). But the analysis does not stop there. Having delineated the steps, the CX team looks at how the customer feels throughout the process at various touchpoints, as well as what points of contact the customer is actually interacting with (for example, a website, an app, or a customer service rep). Then the team looks at the systems that power those points of contact (such as a scheduling system, a customer system, or an application used by the customer service rep). Those systems may in turn depend on other systems.

This exercise may reveal, for example, that a bottleneck in some system three levels deep is the ultimate cause of the customer's challenges. A cursory analysis might lead a decision-maker to suggest, "Yes, let's just build an app to make this easier." But until the team digs deeper into the systems involved, the root cause of the problem is invisible, and therefore impossible to address.

Another tool for analyzing root causes is the "Five Whys" technique. Each "why" gets at a deeper issue that an enterprise may need to solve. For example, suppose a business services company is attempting to find the root cause of a problem: Profit margins for services are eroding. The Five Whys technique might look like this:

Why are profits eroding? Because the cost of delivering on service contracts is too high relative to contract pricing.

Why are we pricing services too cheaply? Because we sell too many deeply discounted service contracts.

Why are we selling so many deeply discounted service contracts? Because at the end of the quarter, sales teams are incented on the volume of contracts closed, so they discount contracts to close deals to meet their quotas.

Why are sales teams incented on volume of contracts closed? Because our accounting systems are designed to make it easier to calculate sales volume than profit per contract.

Why are the accounting systems designed to calculate sales volume rather than profit? Because they're based on an outdated system that was purchased when the company was much smaller.

This Five Whys analysis thus reveals that a problem that appeared to be related to pricing is actually a complex mix of people (sales teams), processes (quarterly incentive calculations), and technology (accounting systems). Until the organization makes improvements at the root cause level—in this case, a failure to budget improvements to the accounting system—the profitability issue will persist.

CLASSICAL SYSTEMS THINKING AND THE ICEBERG MODEL

The concept of systems thinking is more than fifty years old. It originated at MIT, where one of its foremost proponents was Daniel H. Kim, cofounder of the MIT Center for Organizational Learning.

Start with the idea of a system. What distinguishes a system from other collections of objects or processes is interdependence and purpose. According to Kim, "A system is any group of interacting, interrelated, interdependent parts that form a complex and unified whole."[24] Systems have a purpose: They are assembled with the intention to accomplish a goal. For the system to achieve that purpose effectively, all parts of the system must be present and interconnected. Fundamentally, systems persist because of feedback: they react to data in ways that allow them to continue to fulfill their purposes.

These basic properties belie the complexity involved in analyzing systems like companies and economies. That complexity arises not just from the interconnectedness of elements of the system, but especially from their inherent feedback mechanisms. In all corporate systems, feedback to maintain stability is a key element. When sales are in decline, organizations change products or marketing to compensate. When competitors cut into market share, organizations may ramp up advertising. When labor costs cut into profits, organizations may increase prices or lower operating expenses to compensate.

But understanding that feedback is present is just the beginning. In Kim's treatment of systems thinking, the goal is to understand four layers of significance within any system and its behaviors. Kim calls this analysis "the iceberg" because it looks beneath the surface at root causes and models (see figure 7-1).

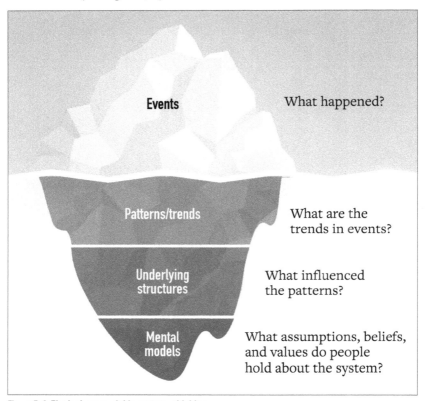

Figure 7-1. The iceberg model in systems thinking.

These are the four layers:

1. **Events.** What happened? What does the data show? In the business services profitability example we used in the previous section, the precipitating event might be a quarterly report that details lower profitability. Enterprises react to such events, but short-term reactions do nothing to address the underlying causes of the problem.

2. **Patterns and trends.** What is the historical context? In the business services example, the trend is toward lower profits each quarter. Having detected a pattern, decision-makers may use this trend to anticipate the future ("We need to prepare for another decline in profitability."). But anticipating future events, while it generates more understanding, again fails to treat the deeper problem.

3. **Underlying structures.** How are elements of the system contributing to the pattern? In the business services example, the systems of incentives for salespeople are contributing to the profitability problem. This level of insight reveals more about what's going on, and it may lead corporate problem-solvers to design improvements to the system. But tinkering with the system is often insufficient to fix stubborn organizational problems.

4. **Mental models.** True understanding begins with a model of what's happening in the organization—a model that includes all the parts, how they are connected, and how people, processes, and technology interact to generate events, patterns, and structures. In the business services example, the model would include the salespeople's incentive programs, the company's attitudes toward sales compensation, the way contracts contribute to profitability, and, crucially, the accounting systems that power the compensation model. Mental models are deeply rooted and culturally persistent. Changing them requires that executives transform the business. This is the most difficult part of systems

thinking, but it gets at the root causes that drive the more easily perceived events, patterns, and structures.

THE SIX ELEMENTS OF CORPORATE SYSTEMS

The normal lens for analyzing corporate systems focuses on three elements: people, processes, and technology. But to get a full view of root causes requires adding a perspective on three other elements: service and product delivery, partners and ecosystems, and governance and performance frameworks. For effective insight, it's critical to define how these six business capabilities come together to deliver value to your customers. So let's take a closer look at each of these six elements, the role they play in systems, and the perspective they can yield in any transformation effort.

People and organization

Enterprises may be systems, but they are not machines. The most important element in any enterprise is the human element: the people contributing to it.

When analyzing a system—or an entire enterprise—start by reviewing the current management structure. This includes the organizational structure as well as current roles and responsibilities. Assess the capabilities of those staff and how they contribute to the system. Then identify the highest priority initiatives that are absorbing the largest share of key human resources.

For example, at ClinicCo, as described in chapter 2, an understanding of the roles and responsibilities of the workers in the clinics was essential to any planned improvement—as was the way responsibility was assigned both in each clinic and across the organization.

Changes that affect staff could include realigning responsibilities of managers, implementing flexible workforce models, reorganizing, or outsourcing. Consider how transforming a corporate system might have differing impacts on different types of workers. Recognize where there are gaps in the capabilities of staff that you could address by investing in training or changing the skills you hire for. These sorts of changes can powerfully impact human resources departments, so consider what sort of HR and management models are appropriate to get desired productivity from the workforce.

Process

Any carefully considered systems perspective examines process: how work gets done. This starts with identifying key process areas and who is responsible for them across the organization.

For example, the development methods at TechCo that we detailed in chapter 5 featured a waterfall process that kept design, engineering, and testing separate. These processes were a root cause of the organization's inability to respond to change in its product design. A more responsive organization there required a shift to Agile development processes.

There are many options for process improvement; a smart executive will match the improvement to the objective of the transformation. An enterprise could move to reduce complexity, introduce intelligent process automation, redesign processes in accordance with Lean principles, or implement business process outsourcing.

Process changes can be almost as contentious as people changes, since they impact everything about how people do their work. A systems perspective here is essential, since changes in process can have unexpected impacts—and because old ways of working have a way of stubbornly reasserting themselves. Leaning heavily on data in these instances can be very beneficial. Data is the truth. It helps remove emotion from the equation so people can chart a clear path forward.

Technology

At this point, technology is a pervasive part of every corporate system. Some technology enables some people and processes to go forward smoothly in furtherance of the organization's goals, while flaws in other technology often hinder people's ability to get work done collaboratively and productively.

For example, as we'll describe in more detail in chapter 10, a credit union found itself unable to score and approve loans at a pace appropriate to its commitment to its customers. The employees were eager to go forward, but the technical systems used to evaluate customers and loans were unable to scale to meet the organization's needs. A rigorous evaluation of all the processes and systems involved clearly identified the need to replace the loan origination system with one from a new vendor: a major development effort, but a necessary one for the credit union to meet its goals.

Evaluation of technology is challenging because there are so many integrated technical systems involved in any medium or large enterprise. These might include systems for worker collaboration, customer relationship management systems, databases, inventory systems, computer-aided design systems, mobile apps, security systems, financial applications . . . the list is virtually endless. Any one of these systems, or the interactions between them, could be a root cause of challenges the enterprise faces. (Recall the accounting system at the root of the profitability problem we described earlier in this chapter.)

Recognize as well that all these systems are continually generating data—often data that the organization needs to make decisions. The integrity of that data—and the ability to visualize it and use it in feedback loops, as we'll describe in chapter 9—is often an element of systems analysis and can be a critical indicator of where you are facing challenges.

Modernizing such technology is often essential to solving systems problems. This might include not just improving software, but also replacing it to address problems with its architecture, modularity, flexibility, data integrity, efficiency, or cost. Given the pace of change in business, software that can't easily be updated and adapted is at the root of many a corporate challenge.

Service and product delivery

When there are problems at the interface between the enterprise and its customers, trouble soon follows. Consider telecom companies that appear to do well until you need service, or retailers who are fine at selling but fall apart at processing returns. For these reasons, we separate out service and product delivery as a separate one of the six enterprise elements to analyze as part of systems thinking. Reviewing this element is a way to focus on the fundamental importance of customer centricity.

The credit union in chapter 3 provides a fine example. It recognized that customers who wanted to dispute debit card charges were having a poor, disjointed experience that reflected badly on the credit union. Until that element of the banking experience was improved, the full system that was the credit union could not provide customers with the complete service they deserved.

In chapter 3, we described multiple strategies to dig into root causes of service and product delivery issues. The customer journey mapping exercise we defined earlier in this chapter is another method. Tracing back to identify the sources of delivery quality and customer satisfaction issues is essential to systems thinking. So is building and maintaining a framework for constantly monitoring customer experience and a workflow for addressing issues. There's a mindset issue here as well; customer centricity only works if it becomes a value shared by the entire organization, even in functional groups that never actually interact with customers.

Partners and ecosystems

The systems that matter in companies don't stop at corporate boundaries. Relationships with suppliers are consequential, as car companies found out in 2021 when they were unable to source necessary microprocessors. So are wholesale and retail relationships for manufacturers.

Many successful companies now exist in the midst of a cloud of vendors of add-ons and services. It's not just Google and Apple that have app stores. The farm equipment maker John Deere, for example, succeeds in part because a network of software companies, data suppliers, and service vendors extends the value of its products. And some companies, like Salesforce, are built on a foundation of partnership ecosystems.

In chapter 9, for example, we'll describe how the health network OhioHealth reengineered its intranet to enable its workers to be more productive—and to enhance its ability to remain compliant with health regulations. Its improvements were dependent, not just on its software supplier Microsoft SharePoint, but also on all of the various health insurers, pharmaceutical companies, and suppliers of medical devices that had to be integrated into the way its professionals served patients.

As a result, an evaluation of partners, suppliers, and other ecosystem players must be part of every analysis of corporate systems. Improvements may include managing partners better, sourcing new vendors, or identifying other solution providers. Homegrown technical systems are becoming increasingly hard to maintain, causing many organizations to adopt customized off-the-shelf solutions and cloud-based software as a service (SaaS). The quality and responsiveness of the vendors supplying those solutions must be part of every analysis of systems and problems.

Governance and performance frameworks

Rules define systems. This includes rules that define how companies operate, regulatory requirements, and, especially, incentives used to reward workers—like the sales incentives in the business services example we started the chapter with.

At the travel company we described in chapter 1, there was no effective governance framework. Applications were developed in a siloed fashion and departments wielded power in ways that were poorly aligned with the goals of the organization. The result, unsurprisingly, was an organization that failed to adapt to change—in this case, the surge of demand that arose as the pandemic receded. A systems thinking perspective would reveal that the lack of governance was largely responsible.

Analyzing governance and performance frameworks starts with identifying where in the organization value is coming from, as we described in the previous chapter. Consider how the organization reports results, how it measures KPIs, and what dashboards it uses to keep tabs on performance. Is the organization transparent about the dimensions on which it performs well or poorly and the measures it uses to evaluate those dimensions? Does it use analytics to identify what's working and where problems are arising? And how do all those measurements feed into employees' and managers' financial rewards?

Improving not just what you measure, but how you share it and how you use it to influence behavior in service of the right goals is a key element in any transformation effort.

Although these six elements appear to be separate, they interact constantly as part of the system of your organization. When you make a change in any area, you need to adjust the system. Consider how the process and technology of intelligent automation may have an impact on people and organization. Analysis of people and their roles must include how they will work with automated processes, both now and in the future. Alternatively, do you need a partner to help deliver on the promise? Are your customers expecting AI or automation to drive greater functionality or a better customer experience? How do you govern AI models to avoid bias? The questions themselves are not as important as the process of questioning the impact of any one change on all of the six elements in the system.

TENURE AND INERTIA

There's another consideration that should go into every systems thinking exercise: an analysis of inertia that may hold back change. Where does inertia come from?

One staffing leader has a theory. Rob Ganjon is CEO of Cella, a Randstad operating company that is a leader in consulting, staffing, and managed solutions for creative, marketing, digital, and proposal development teams. His observation is that the most important source of inertia is people who are stuck in their jobs for too long.

In Rob's view, institutional inertia is composed of the aggregated inertia of all the individuals in a company. Those individuals don't start their work with inertia. Rob's core insight is that inertia is correlated with each individual's tenure in their role.

Here's his explanation:

I've seen a similar pattern emerge time and time again. When a person lands in a new role (either as an external hire, an internal transfer, or through a promotion), they generally come in with a lot of energy. They are excited and want to make an impact. And, by definition, they are seeing things with a fresh perspective because it's new to them. The first 12 to 18 months are filled with new ideas and innovation occurs organically. However, after two or three years in the role, that excitement and level of innovation starts to wane. The individual's energy starts to shift towards optimizing their work to meet their personal goals, which is usually some version of maximizing ROI on their effort.

I'm sure we can all relate to this dynamic. You've been in the role a few years. You have a good team in place. Things are working well. You have a nice routine and it's comfortable. You know well how to meet expectations and the job is pleasant. At this point, change (whether it's initiated by you or by someone else) comes with a lot of risk—both to your ability to continue meeting expectations as well as your ability to remain comfortable in your routine. And this is when you start resisting change. Inertia has set in. Once you have large portions of your workforce with three-plus years of tenure in-role, your risk of institutional inertia is high.

Systemically, of course, you can't change people's tenure—you can only acknowledge that tenure is a factor. But you can chip away at it by moving people around, hiring people with new ideas, and, where necessary, moving aside or cutting ties with people who have proven more adept at defending their status quo than solving the organization's actual problems. You could even place limits on allowable tenure in a given job. As Rob explains, "At a high-growth company, this culture of people movement and innovation happens naturally as a result of the high rate of growth. At slower-growth companies, the culture of people movement needs to be implemented deliberately."

There is a popular articulation of this philosophy: Lead, follow, or get out of the way. In any transformation, these are the behaviors that matter. Leaders are excited about the transformation and will help to make it happen. Followers are less excited, but willing to participate. Those whose jobs are unaffected can, for the most part, get out of the way. But anybody else becomes an impediment—and if they won't be won over, they must be moved around or out.

TOOLS FOR SYSTEMS THINKING

While you can acquire the attitude of systems thinking, it's not a simple technique you can just apply to any change or project. Instead, consider embracing systems thinking using a variety of methods to get at the root causes of problems. Taken together, these tools can elevate your thinking above the easy but ultimately unproductive surface solutions that come most quickly to mind.

That list of methods you can use for systems thinking include any of the following (each listed with the chapters where we describe them in more detail):

- **Design thinking.** Systematically generate and test ideas for addressing customer needs (chapter 3).

- **Defining operating models and operational road maps.** Describe the operation of the enterprise and all of its elements, along with desired changes, in a holistic fashion (chapter 4).

- **Organizational change management.** Plan a systematic rollout of changes, addressing how managers and staff will learn to lead or participate (chapter 4).

- **Aligning governance and measurement with value.** Revise the rules under which the enterprise operates and the data that powers them (chapter 4).

- **Adopting Lean principles.** Identify and root out waste. (chapter 5).

- **Analyzing processes with a product mindset.** Define features, outcomes, and improvements of processes as if they were products and thus enable agile development (chapter 5).

- **Analyzing where value in the organization is generated.** Perform a detailed value analysis as preparation for aligning investments with value (chapter 6).

- **Journey mapping.** Identify root causes of customer experience challenges (earlier in this chapter).

- **The Five Whys.** Reveal root causes of surface problems (earlier in this chapter).
- **Identifying the mental models that drive the organization.** Use the iceberg model to find how mental models influence organizational behavior (earlier in this chapter).
- **Leveraging empowered teams.** Use cross-functional teams to gain insights that aren't visible within corporate silos (chapter 8).
- **Analyzing the arc of value.** Recognize the maturity of efforts and how data can be applied based on what stage of development they are in (chapter 9).
- **Designing feedback loops.** Use systems theory to collect data and integrate course corrections into the function of the organization (chapter 9).
- **Assessing core technology systems.** Identify where technology is powering or impeding innovation and aligning investments and management of that technology accordingly (chapter 10).

By applying these tools appropriately, you can get at the leverage points that will make any transformation more likely to succeed.

Systems thinking looks at the organization as a whole. But change originates at the lowest level, where teams are getting the work done. We examine empowered teams in the next chapter.

Chapter 8

EMPOWER TEAMS TO IMPROVE SKILLS AND MAKE DECISIONS

In August of 2020, Ryan Hatcher changed jobs. After more than a decade as a fundraiser at the Leukemia & Lymphoma Society (LLS), a nonprofit charity serving people with blood cancers, he accepted an offer from the organization to be vice president of strategy and innovation. And it was a good time to be innovative.

LLS raises more than $400 million per year from charitable gifts and other contributions. Much of that comes from marathons, triathlons, walks, stair climbs, and hikes in which volunteers participate to raise money for the organization. The organization then applies those funds to help individuals with blood cancers and to support scientific research; three-fourths of FDA-approved blood cancer treatments were developed in part through research supported by LLS.

When Hatcher changed jobs in 2020, everything about how LLS worked was being upended by COVID. Cancer patients were starting to wonder if checkups were risky and if vaccines were safe or effective for people in their condition. Canceled athletic events threatened to put a dent in LLS fundraising. And the organization's hundreds of employees, many of whom were now working from home, needed to find new ways to work together.

Ryan teamed up with three other employees, hired another, and then began to invest in learning ways to innovate effectively. One of those methods was design thinking, the method we described in chapter 3 that is based on five steps: empathizing with customers, defining problems in novel ways, ideating new solutions, prototyping those solutions, and testing the results. Similar to the Agile methods we describe in chapter 5, design thinking moves forward in rapid sprints of a week or two, iterating on possible solutions.

Ryan and his team worked with us on a particular challenge: reaching college students. The nonprofit was interested in ways to support college students who had survived childhood blood cancers and in connecting those affected by blood cancers in their families for both support and fundraising.

Those initial innovation experiments surfaced promising ideas for engaging with college students, including recruiting gamers as sponsors.

More importantly, though, they lit the spark of innovation in Ryan's new team. And LLS management kindled that spark. Connecting with employees and volunteers throughout the organization, Ryan's team invented some startling new ways to benefit those with blood cancers, even in the throes of the COVID-19 pandemic.

In one breakthrough program, LLS began a national patient registry. Patients could contribute their health information, including the state of their blood cancers, their COVID infection status, and their vaccination history. The registry aggregated this information, stripping out patient identifiers, and made it available to researchers to study the critical and urgent question of how COVID and vaccines affect people with blood cancers.

Ryan's group created other innovations designed to adapt the organization to a post-COVID world. These included virtual fundraisers that allowed volunteers to stage shared events like stair climbs, even in situations where they couldn't safely gather together in large groups.

Ryan's progress was rapid. Small teams, empowered by organizations to respond to challenges like COVID patient support and fundraising, and trained in disciplines like design thinking, make incredible leaps ahead. This energy holds the secret that every organization needs to become responsive—if it can embrace the sometimes challenging idea of empowering teams.

THE CHALLENGE OF RESPONSIVENESS AT SCALE

Why bother with empowered teams at all? Couldn't a traditionally organized enterprise be equally responsive?

Not really. The challenge arises from traditional organizational design. Large enterprises have grown in ways that deal most effectively with static conditions. They are organized by functions. Design departments design. Engineering departments engineer. Marketing departments market and sales departments sell.

In theory, these groups can all work together to serve the customer. But in practice, this organizational structure tends to create silos. Politically, functional groups have incentives to cling to budget dollars and favor their own work over that of other functional groups. Functions attempt to maximize their own success, even when that effort creates excess demands on other groups in the company. They hoard data, head count, and opportunity. The need to collaborate with others is "overhead," consuming time and resources that subtract from the department's "core" work.

IT departments have a particular challenge here, since they're held responsible for infrastructure and risk, often working far from the point at which customers interact with the company. This mindset is what creates the traditionally conservative and slow-moving culture of IT, a group that's continually asked to do more with less. In such organizations, there's little incentive for IT to take risks and be responsive on behalf of customers. We describe one good way to address this problem in chapter 10.

Obviously, organizations still do collaborate and produce value for customers. But this collaboration tends to happen in rigidly defined ways that can't flex at the speed of change in today's environment. When groups do collaborate on product road maps, a department becomes responsible for features in a fixed plan, not customer outcomes in a dynamic environment. Organizations reward functional teams for production, not responsiveness. And so the organization continues to lurch ahead, with scale as its main advantage—an advantage that becomes an impediment when conditions change.

There are bright spots in any organization: people like Ryan Hatcher who creatively attempt to do the right thing for customers and other stakeholders. They will often reach out to like-minded staff and attempt to respond in ways that, frankly, require them to evade management structures. But ad-hoc, side-of-desk innovation that's contrary to organizational culture and incentives doesn't scale.

EMPOWERED, CROSS-FUNCTIONAL TEAMS ARE FAR MORE RESPONSIVE

The solution to this challenge is based on a simple but profound insight: Small, cross-functional teams can be far more responsive to customer needs than large, monolithic departments. The shift to empowered teams isn't easy, but the payoff is enormous. And that shift can happen at scale, and without unnecessary chaos, if you manage it properly.

The empowered team framework does not require a reorganization of reporting relationships. Engineers will still report into a head of engineering, marketers to a head of marketing, and so on. But those staffers are now assigned to cross-functional teams with specific objectives. For example, a team dedicated to check deposits and money transfers in a mobile banking app might include a customer experience expert, a marketer, a designer, an engineer or two, a security expert, and someone expert in interfaces to back-office operations. Each of those professionals would still report to their respective supervisors, but their day-to-day work would focus on ways to improve the function of mobile check deposits and money transfers.

The cross-functional makeup of such teams is essential because it enables rapid progress and systems awareness. Imagine the mobile banking team again. The customer experience expert has the best knowledge of what the customer wants, but that must be tempered with growth and profit goals as articulated by the marketing person. The designer and engineer can collaborate on ways to deliver the benefit, while the security staffer suggests how to make the features resistant to hacking, and the back-office expert analyzes what's feasible in connecting to corporate systems. A proposed advance makes sense only when the whole team contributes from their various perspectives. And as they learn from each other's perspectives, the team members become more mature in ideating and assessing potential improvements that benefit the company and contribute to the company's vision. An empowered cross-functional team can grow and make strides at an accelerated pace because it can do what is most effective without waiting for permission from management of one function or another.

In a large organization, there could be hundreds of such teams. Each team must have a customer-focused objective—where the "customer" could be any group being served. The customers of the mobile banking app team are the bank's actual customers. But an infrastructure team might treat the rest of the company's employee base as the customers. In the case of Ryan Hatcher's innovation team, one set of customers could be blood cancer patients, while others could be charitable donors or medical researchers. What matters is that the team focuses on improving the experience of a particular set of end users that are important to the organization.

Empowered teams are most effective when they are small—no more than seven to ten people. Jeff Bezos at Amazon was an adherent of the "two-pizza rule"—every internal team should be small enough that two pizzas would be sufficient to feed them.[25] As Chris DeBrusk wrote in *MIT Sloan Management Review*, "One way to improve the effectiveness of projects is to reduce the size of the teams mobilized to tackle them. In other words, it might be time to make your project teams smaller."[26] DeBrusk points out that smaller teams can build trust, make decisions quickly, and iterate solutions at a higher cadence.

One influential recipe for empowered teams comes from Marty Cagan, a partner at Silicon Valley Product Group and author of the popular 2020 book *Empowered: Ordinary People, Extraordinary Products.* Cagan's vision for empowered teams is focused on technology companies, and, in his model, the teams are all product teams. As he writes, "the purpose of the product team *is to serve customers by creating products customers love, yet work for the business.*"27 And as he clearly states, they "are given *problems to solve*, rather than features to build, and are *empowered to solve these problems in the best way they see fit.* And then they are held accountable for the results."28

While our version of empowered teams isn't solely product-focused, this description gets at the essential elements of the empowered team framework. The focus is on serving customers. Teams are given the authority to solve those customer problems, rather than being told exactly what to do. This requires senior managers to give up much of their immediate control over the work people do on a day-to-day basis, since the teams will not be behaving in completely predictable ways doing completely predictable work. But such an empowering mindset enables the teams to be far more responsive and collaborative, moving much faster in service to customer needs.

MANAGING EMPOWERED TEAMS

The objective here is to create teams that do the right thing because they know it is the right thing to do, rather than sitting around waiting for higher-ups to make decisions. As the venture capitalist John Doerr commented about great companies, they are led by missionaries, not mercenaries—they create a passion in their followers to contribute to the company's mission and vision.29

As we described in chapter 6, a transformational shift like this demands a vision of the value to be delivered, clearly communicated from the top. Organizational leaders must set customer-centric goals, proselytize the value of responsiveness, and create and spread the cultural motivation behind the shift to an empowered team framework. That vision extends to goals and incentives to make sure that the empowered team efforts aren't just layered on top of old, traditional, department-centered ways of doing business.

Senior leaders give something up here: command and control. But they still lead. That starts with articulating the vision, and setting the culture, to keep people working on the right objectives. Leaders set those objectives, determining which teams to create and what problems to turn them loose on. The goals should be outcome-based, for example, "grow the customer base by 10% per year," or "reduce downtime by 50%." Those are very different types of goals from command-and-control-focused activity-based goals ("Make 100 phone calls per week" or "Write 200 lines of code per month"). Outcome-based, customer-focused goals empower the teams, maximizing responsiveness and productivity by clearly defining leadership's objectives for the team, rather than dictating the exact methods used to accomplish those objectives.

One challenge for managers is that at first, empowered teams may actually appear less productive than teams with a strong, directive leader. But according to management research from business school professors Natalia M. Lorinkova, Matthew J. Pearsall, and Henry P. Sims Jr., the performance of empowered teams rises to surpass teams with a directive leader after the teams have been working together for a while.[30] "Empowering leadership tends to create psychological ownership of a task, heightened efficacy and commitment, and higher levels of coordination and collective information processing," they write. These researchers attribute the improvement to collective team learning, coordination of behaviors, a psychological feeling of empowerment, and development of shared mental models.

Leaders can contribute to a strong start for empowered teams by creating a center of excellence for empowered teams within the organization. This facility trains new teams in the new responsibilities and interactions they will share and in what management now expects in the new model—learning which is essential for the team to develop and work effectively. The center of excellence is also available to answer questions as the team gets its feet under it.

After the team is running and being productive, what role does a leader play? Based on a study of 300 self-managing teams at a Fortune 500 company, professors Vanessa Urch Druskat and Jane V. Wheeler concluded that "the best external leaders were not necessarily the ones who had adopted a hands-off approach, nor were they simply focused on encouraging team members in various ways. Instead, the external leaders who had contributed most to their team's success excelled at one skill: managing the boundary between the team and the larger organization."[31] This included building relationships between the team and the broader organization; scouting out conditions that could benefit or threaten the team; persuading senior managers and the team members to stay the course; removing blockers; and empowering the team by delegating authority and coaching individual team members.

TEAMS MUST GROW TO BECOME PRODUCTIVE

Unsurprisingly, just plopping down an empowered team to solve a problem doesn't immediately pay off, because the team takes a while to connect, learn to collaborate, and work productively together. A center of excellence and empowerment from leadership can take the team to the starting line, but they have to run the race themselves.

A useful way to think about what happens with the growth of empowered teams is the four-stage model developed by the psychologist Bruce W. Tuckman: forming, storming, norming, and performing.[32]

- In the **forming** stage, the group begins to define its identity. This starts with the selection of team members from different functional groups. If hiring is necessary, focus on mindset as much as skills; customer-focused, clever, collaborative problem solvers are better than narrow specialists. In this stage, enthusiasm is high, but the team is as focused on getting to know how to work together as it is on actually solving problems.

- In the **storming** stage, the team is solving problems—and grappling with actual obstacles. Since the empowered team methods are new, teams often struggle with just how much autonomy is appropriate and may from time to time slide back to permission-seeking behavior. On the other hand, this is when the team develops the collaboration behaviors that can lead to startling customer-focused advances.

- In the **norming** stage, the team becomes more comfortable with its role and the roles of individual participants. This allows a shift in focus to recognizing the creativity of individuals' ideas for solutions and in actually achieving the team's objectives. A string of successes at this stage lays the groundwork for the team's ascendance to high performance.

- In the **performing** stage, the group recognizes its collective potency and develops larger ambitions for achieving its overall goals. Team members anticipate each other's contributions, allowing for a regular and predictable set of advances. Members may leave or be promoted, but as new members join the team, they'll be stepping into established roles and can quickly become productive.

Once you recognize this cycle, you can embrace it to spread effective empowered teams throughout the organization. Don't start with thirty teams. Start with one or two, working on problems where there is an obvious need. Those first few teams and the center of excellence will learn from each other. As you then spin up other teams, they can benefit from the experience of the first few teams; teams that have begun norming or performing can help train teams that are forming or storming.

When empowered teams hit their stride, they make major contributions to company productivity and employee retention. As the business school professors' research we cited earlier confirmed, teams that stay together spend more time in the productive performing stage. It can be beneficial to keep the team intact even when a project ends. Struggling through the forming, storming, and norming stages each time you need a new team is inefficient; better to take advantage of people with a great working relationship, even if it's on a new project.

INNOVATION AND EMPOWERED TEAMS GO HAND IN HAND

So far, the teams we've spent the most time on are those that management assigns to existing, established objectives and initiatives. But how do empowered teams figure in the generation of new and innovative programs outside of the organization's core ways of doing business?

Ryan Hatcher at LLS shows one clue: It's possible to set up a team empowered specifically to innovate new ideas. That's a great way to start with empowerment.

But innovative ideas often pop up all over the organization. How is it possible to empower those innovators to get new initiatives started?

In the Harvard Business Review Press book *Empowered: Unleash Your Employees, Energize Your Customers, Transform Your Business*, Josh Bernoff and Ted Schadler suggest a plan for this. It's called the HERO compact (HERO is an acronym for highly empowered and resourceful operative), and it involves three groups: management, IT, and potential innovators hoping to exploit new technologies, also known as HEROes.[33] Management must agree to identify, vet, and empower innovators with resources. Because those innovations, left unchecked, can sometimes threaten security, IT's role in the HERO compact is to support those innovators, but help put up guardrails to keep them safe. In this scenario, innovators must commit to work in ways that support the company's business goals and live within the guardrails put up by IT.

Company leaders could commit to build new empowered teams around these innovators' ideas, as they did with Ryan Hatcher at the Leukemia & Lymphoma Society. But in a large organization, how can you identify such innovators?

The most innovative ideas happen across departmental boundaries—customer experience experts with engineering ideas, for example, or IT staff who realize something new is possible in marketing. Those cross-boundary ideas can be awkward to find and embrace, and there's a risk that they just end up falling through the cracks.

One way to highlight these ideas is with innovation management software like Imaginatik or Planview's IdeaPlace, software that functions like a social media environment for new ideas. Employees contribute new ideas, and others comment on, add to, or critique those ideas. The most interesting ideas tend to go viral within the company, rising to the top of the innovation management software's threads.

According to an article by Bernoff and two others in *Harvard Business Review* online, data from 3.5 million employees using innovation management software shows that four variables predict the ideation rate at a company: scale (number of participants), frequency (the number of ideas suggested), engagement (the number of people responding to ideas), and diversity (the types of people making suggestions).[34]

It's not much of a stretch to put that all together and see that a culture of empowerment—one in which new ideas are revered and innovators across the company are empowered—leads to a high rate of ideation. Leaders can reward those innovators with their own cross-functional teams, which will function alongside the other empowered teams, generating new customer-focused ideas.

To fully exploit the power of empowered teams, companies must put in place feedback loops that help guide them to iterate in productive directions. That's the topic of the next chapter.

Chapter 9

EMBED FEEDBACK LOOPS IN SYSTEMS AND ACT ON DATA

Sometimes obsolescing technology systems challenge an organization. You can look at that as a problem, or you can seize it as an opportunity to make continuous improvement.

That's what happened at OhioHealth, one of the largest health care providers in the US, with thirteen hospitals, more than 200 ambulatory sites, and 35,000 employees.

Melissa Young was responsible for internal communication in the intranet site for OhioHealth. Her role was challenging because the subject matter of questions the intranet could answer spanned such a wide range of topics, from employment questions like "What's the policy for paid time off?" to medical questions like "What's the right procedure to prepare a patient to insert a breathing tube?" For employees, or as OhioHealth calls them, associates, finding answers takes time. Shorten the time between the question and the answer, and you've improved the work of an associate. Do that for the questions asked thousands of times, and you've enabled the entire organization to spend more time providing care, rather than searching in vain to find answers buried somewhere in the organization's archives.

Melissa's challenge at OhioHealth started with technology modernization for the organization's intranet, known as eSource, which was supposed to house the answers to associates' most common questions. The update was required because eSource was operating on an aging instance of Microsoft's intranet platform, SharePoint.

But the technology modernization wouldn't fix eSource's biggest problem: usability. As Melissa told us, "Associates said it was hard to find information, and what was there was often duplicated, inaccurate, or outdated. It was a frustrating experience." Melissa's team was hearing the same sorts of complaints from nurses, nutritionists, physicians, and finance people. All relied on eSource, but they disdained the actual site experience.

Melissa quickly realized that just shoveling the 2.3 terabytes of information from the old eSource into a new intranet would accomplish little. Instead, she seized the opportunity to completely revamp how OhioHealth communicated with and served its staff. While health care is rarely a sector where change happens quickly, she recognized that a rapid and major improvement could significantly improve the way that staff conducted their work every day.

The work started with assembling a team and gathering data.

The new eSource team would include staff from Melissa's internal communications group, OhioHealth's Change Management group, and the company's IT department, which maintained the workforce's technology. It also included outside technology implementation contractors for implementation and consultants from Celerity.

To start with baseline data, Melissa's team did extensive interviews with all sorts of users—physicians, nurses, and nonclinical staff—and conducted a broad associate survey that generated more than 5,000 responses.

The team decided to go forward with an Agile methodology, starting with a minimum viable product and improving it with rapid development sprints. The first objective was to create an intranet that was very fast and very efficient in delivering information for the top ten employee needs, as well as a way to allow the leaders in the organization to communicate quickly with all the staff.

According to Melissa, this Agile development process felt very different from her past projects. "The difference was the product mindset," she explained. "We were able to establish eSource as a product and maintain it as a product."

In the design sprints, the team updated portions of the eSource prototype and tested them with small sets of typical users. It also designed a series of templates to make it easy for owners of different content areas to quickly create consistently formatted content for what they anticipated would be the answers to the most asked user questions. The prototype went through six or seven iterations informed by quick user tests and revisions.

Once the minimum viable product was ready, the team rolled it out to all associates and continued to make improvements in more two-week design sprints. The focus all along was on making significant, steady improvements. "We were constantly changing navigation, creating new content that didn't exist before," Melissa explained. "We were responding to user questions: associates searching for what to do about jury duty, for example. We were identifying the content that people needed most."

Rapid development like this depends on feedback loops. This meant carefully examining data as soon as each release went live. The team collected data on qualitative and quantitative metrics from the site, including these:

- Data returned by the search function: What were associates seeking?
- Completion rate of tasks: Did the user find what they were seeking?
- Completion times: How long did tasks take?
- User errors per task: How often did user queries fail?
- Abandonment: Did patterns emerge in click paths where users abandoned the process?

- Problems per user, both information architecture problems and user interface problems

Even as such metrics informed the design direction, the team also collected data on the site's long-term success, including:

- Usage statistics for eSource
- Net Promoter Score for eSource
- Reduction in calls to technical support

The quantitative feedback helped fend off ad-hoc requests for change, like groups that used to have a button on the home page and were disappointed to no longer be represented so prominently in the interface. "We had data to show where they fell in relation to other tasks; that conversation was easier, because you had data to make smart decisions," Melissa explained, "versus deciding based on who had the loudest voice or could ladder up to the highest person in the organization." As in so many other cases, data establishes the objective truth.

In addition to these quantitative results, the team conducted and often recorded video of actual users attempting to use the product. This proved essential, because there's nothing like a user attempting a task, getting stuck, and then describing their frustration to impress a developer on the need to change the design of a pet feature.

The combination of convincing data and regular user testing enabled the rapid evolution of eSource in productive directions, and not always in ways that the team would have anticipated at first. The top five priorities for development would often change from sprint to sprint as user needs evolved.

The feedback loops generated measurable progress. Time spent on the site per session decreased—a positive metric, since it meant people could identify the information they needed and then get back to their jobs. The number of clicks to find information shrank. And the utilization of five key content areas continued to increase, just as the designers had anticipated.

These differences were also accompanied by a complete change in attitude among users. Instead of hearing "IT does not have capacity for your project," employees were seeing the site change within days of their requests for new features. User satisfaction rose dramatically. On the clinical site, employees got far quicker access to information they needed to deliver care. Finance found the site to be far better at getting policies and information published and in front of staff.

In a staid industry like health care, when a product moves rapidly in a positive direction, users get excited. That kind of improvement demands data and a system to review it regularly and take advantage of what you learn. As Melissa put it, "If you are making all of these decisions with broad well-developed user insight based on data, there is very little argument, and many more conversations about how to move forward."

Rapid development is never an end in itself. The point is not just speed, but speed in a productive direction. And as Melissa learned, feedback loops are how you ensure and then prove that the direction of development is what's most beneficial for users at every stage.

RAPID PROGRESS DEPENDS ON FEEDBACK LOOPS

Consider a race car driver. At each moment while driving, the driver is getting information about the effect of decisions they make. Gauges reflect speed, RPMs, engine temperature, and whether they're about to run out of gas. They also get feedback moment by moment from the feel of the car, as well as voices in their headset from team members with a different perspective.

Without all that feedback, it's unsafe to go fast. All that data allows for constant adjustment. Without it, as a driver, you'd never know where you'd end up.

OhioHealth moved forward rapidly and effectively on its intranet because Melissa and the team there had planned for constant feedback—measurements of usage and error rates, insights from regular user tests, and questions from actual users in the field. Every couple of weeks they could implement course corrections based on actual data, ensuring that they were moving closer to a tool that would actually help their internal customers do their jobs. And on a longer time frame, the project also had metrics that allowed the team to prove its worth to those who funded and managed it.

The changing development priorities from week to week could be challenging, but teams working in a responsive enterprise must embrace the fact that they don't know all requirements right out of the gate, and they may even be surprised by some of the changing priorities and requirements along the way. Ultimately, though, an agile and responsive attitude results in better products.

But while feedback is an important source of information, it doesn't tell you what to do. The development team needs to temper what they hear with the company's and product's priorities, accepting feedback that indicates a problem many users face, but not necessarily feedback that would become a distraction from the goal of delivering maximum value.

The other challenge with feedback loops is that there are so many possible things to measure. What matters, how should you measure it, and what systems should you set up to act on what you learn? That's what this chapter will describe.

THE ARC OF VALUE

As you consider feedback loops, think about the arc of value and how it changes over a product life cycle.

Historically, the maximum value of a product was at launch or when it rolled off of a production line and was placed on the store shelf. Now, with the increase of data analytics tools and the ability to analyze large amounts of usage data, companies can obtain insights to improve products after they've been designed and delivered, later in the product life cycle. When this feedback is incorporated into the product, the result is a higher percentage of successful products.

This is a fundamental insight for the agile mindset. The notion that we know everything once we complete the project planning and ideation stage of a venture is presumptuous and inefficient. The incremental approach creates better products because the process inherently embraces the fact that we don't know everything and that feedback loops represent the period of most value creation.

Let's look at a product's arc of value with this knowledge in mind (see figure 9-1).

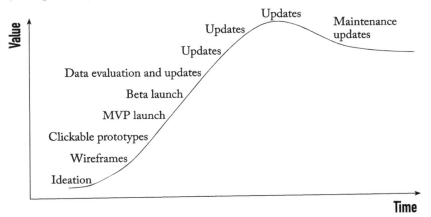

Figure 9-1. The arc of value.

At the start of any project, lots of things are in flux. The value is mostly a promise. And it's hard to measure anything, because nothing's been built yet. Most of the feedback comes from showing potential users wireframes and asking for opinions or perspectives.

Once the project goes live with users, feedback loops begin to generate a big payoff. You put something out there, and if you're measuring the right things, you immediately learn what's working, what's not, and what could be better. You can make improvements on a weekly basis. Feedback loops are crucial at this stage, because when you're moving fastest, a smart improvement can add a lot of value, while a misguided one could set you back—even if it's only a week or two because of the rapid sprints.

For a while, value continues to increase, fueled by those feedback loops. Eventually, the product matures and the benefits reach a plateau of value.

Even at that point, feedback loops are important. They help identify where new problems and opportunities are cropping up, allowing the team to maintain the project so it continues to deliver value. At the point of product maturity, feedback loops will keep you moving forward on the right track and delivering the maximum possible value, but with more incremental improvements and fewer big leaps of value.

As you implement feedback loops, keep the arc of value in mind. Know whether you're attempting rapid progress or maintaining progress already made; design your feedback systems accordingly.

PRINCIPLES OF FEEDBACK LOOP DESIGN

The time to think about feedback and measurement is at the very start of a project, well before you need the feedback to make decisions. You must instrument your technology, plan data collection, conceive dashboards, and design methods to include feedback in your workflow as an integral part of everything you're building. After all, race car designers plan the gauges in the cockpit and the roles of the people talking on the headset when the car is being built and the race is being planned, not while they're in the middle of the race.

How should you think about the design? At a high level, feedback should have these qualities:

- **Aligned.** Tied to operational, people, and process measures that your team and management have agreed upon.

- **Balanced.** Includes both financial and nonfinancial measurements.

- **Baseline-based**. Evaluated relative to a baseline agreed upon by a product manager and key stakeholders.

- **Committed.** Created with full buy-in of everyone involved.

- **Measurable.** Based on a relevant and focused set of measures.

- **Scalable.** Designed to become increasingly useful as the project grows.

- **Simple.** Clearly defined and easily understood.

- **Transparent.** Generated from a clearly revealed process from trusted data sources.

How do you set up feedback loops that obey these principles? Here are some suggestions:

- **Start with a vision for the project.** What would success look like in business terms? Greater sales? Fewer customer service calls? Higher customer satisfaction? Increases in Net Promoter Scores? All the things you measure should ultimately trace back to these high-level improvements. For example, at OhioHealth, fewer user clicks per visit translated to less time wasted and more immediate access to key information, which led to more effective and happier workers and lower support costs. Measuring clicks only mattered because it was tied back to key business goals.

- **Classify feedback data into short- and long-term categories.** Short-term data includes more easily measured metrics like click-through rates, leads, time spent on site, complaints, and abandoned shopping carts. If you're measuring things properly, you can quickly see if changes in application design and direction are working well or where they may be failing. Qualitative user feedback is also a short-term metric that you can act on quickly. Longer-term metrics include measures like revenue, cost, or customer satisfaction. Behavior changes, often measured with employee surveys, are also long-term measures. You'll generally be checking long-term changes monthly or quarterly to justify that your efforts were worthwhile; course corrections from long-term metrics are more likely to be in budget sizes, continued funding, and hires, rather than changes in interface or features.

- **Consider both quantitative and qualitative feedback.** Numerical data is reassuring. At OhioHealth, for example, the raw information about how many people were finding the information they needed rather than giving up after many minutes was helpful to determine if the new eSource was working properly. But build in opportunities for qualitative feedback as well. This includes methods like videos of users observed as they attempt to accomplish their goals. A single remark like "I can't find the 'Submit' button—Oh, wait, it's scrolled off the screen!" could make a major difference in the next revision of an Agile project.

(At OhioHealth, the team sometimes named an on-screen button after the user whose insight led them to create it.)

- **Determine the cadence of data collection and analysis.** Data dashboards are seductive; it's fun for team members to stare at them and feel good or bad about what's working and what's failing. But a disciplined development process has a cadence to it, for example, a cycle of two-week development sprints. Design your data systems so you can collect and analyze data on that cadence. This will allow the team to view and act on specific feedback from users' experience, rather than overreacting to momentary fluctuations in metrics.

- **Identify and streamline access to data sources.** Data collection is not usually as simple as "Dive into that pile of numbers and get what I want." At OhioHealth, for example, data came from a combination of site analytics, usability tests, post-use surveys, and call-center reporting. Each of those pools of data required a separate plan, and some required negotiation with different groups who had collected or maintained control over the data.

- **Learn to live with fast, imperfect data.** Data is always flawed and rarely ideal; making it perfect would often take so many resources and so much time that it would impede the goal of rapid progress. Instead, determine what "quick and dirty" measures you can assemble without causing delays. For example, four or five carefully observed user tests will often reveal the sources of problems or opportunities for improvement; while ten or twenty would be better, they'd be more likely to slow things down than reveal otherwise hidden insights.

- **Weave data from multiple sources together in visualization tools.** One data visualization tool or report can show results from multiple data streams. Such combined visualizations can lead to actionable "aha" insights.

- **Carefully plan how you will communicate data insights to the team.** Don't hoard data. Instead, design a plan to regularly share it with team members in a transparent dashboard, feedback site, or regularly updated progress report. Everyone needs access to the same feedback so they can collaborate on what the feedback means and how to act on it.

- **Build data into workflows.** Don't forget the "loop" part of feedback loops. Build a workflow that includes data review, analysis, and action plans on a regular cadence, typically associated with your regular meetings (for example, development sprints or quarterly management reviews). Include the collection and display of data (and who is responsible for it) in step descriptions. For example, "Analyst collects and reviews the data, analyst reports key actionable information, team discusses action plans relative to data, product manager agrees on desired improvements, analyst commits to measure improvements for next meeting."

THE FOUR KEY ELEMENTS OF ANY METRIC

Based on these general principles, you can create specific metrics. To design a metric, determine four qualities.

First, what business outcome is this metric tied to? For example, in the case of OhioHealth's eSource, a reduction in time spent on the intranet searching for information is tied to employee productivity, which is connected to efficiency.

Second, what is your target? Imagine a success: What would that number look like? At OhioHealth, the target for search time was a reduction of 25% relative to where it was when the project started. The target should be a stretch—if it's too easy, there's nothing to drive continual improvement—but within the conceivable range if the project succeeds.

Third, what is your data source? Unless you can regularly and consistently get access to the data you need, you don't really have an effective metric. At OhioHealth, the calculation of time spent on search came from web analytics from eSource server logs.

Finally, what is the frequency of measurement? Will you measure weekly, monthly, or on some other cadence? For the search metric at OhioHealth, the time spent on search was monitored every two weeks, but also computed at quarterly or six-month intervals to verify ongoing project success. The appropriate cadence of measurement typically depends on sample size—data from many active users generates sufficient volume to support more frequent insights.

Unless you can nail down all four of these qualities, your metrics will not be consistently available for use in feedback loops. And to be useful for feedback, a metric must be ready without fail whenever it's time to close the loop and use it to inform improvements—which is why access to dynamic data is best.

One way to make data from any metric easy to visualize is with a dashboard. Figure 9-2 includes some tips for building an effective dashboard.

 CONSIDER YOUR AUDIENCE

- Determine how the dashboard will be used.
- Identify the information the reader needs to be successful.
- Determine the level of detail needed.
- Consider how exceptions or insights that need action should be highlighted.
- Consider the learned or cultural assumptions that may affect design choices.
- Note what colors mean and how they can be visually interpreted.
- Consider which icons are familiar.

 CHOOSE THE RIGHT DESIGN

- Limit content to fit entirely on one screen.
- Start with the highest level of detail in upper corners of the screen.
- Keep the dashboard simple with three to five key values, charts, or tables.
- Provide adequate context and keep related items near each other.
- Show degrees of change for quick comparisons.
- If detailed tables are needed, place them at the bottom of the dashboard.

 AVOID COMMON VISUALIZATION ISSUES

- Keep in mind that it is difficult for the human brain to interpret circular shapes.
- Be consistent with chart scales on axes, chart dimension ordering, and the colors used for dimension values within charts.
- Don't exceed three or four digits when displaying numbers.
- Don't mix levels of precision and time.
- Don't clutter your charts with data labels that are not needed.

Figure 9-2. Dashboard tips.

AVOIDING PITFALLS AND PROBLEMS

Inevitably, there will be challenges when you design feedback loops and build them into responsive enterprise plans. A lot of the potential problems come from data access and consistency.

Access to data is one problem. Parts of organizations that collect data may be unwilling to make it available for analysis by other parts of the organization, sometimes because hoarding that data is a source of power. For example, lots of data generated by technology products ends up owned by the IT department, which may feel proprietary about collecting and analyzing that data. It's now clear that the best practice is for data to be available and accessible throughout the organization—this is data democratization, which we discuss in more detail in chapter 10. Despite this principle, data is not always available. According to a study by MicroStrategy, only 44% of companies have made data and analytics available to more than half of their organization.[35]

But that access is wasted unless it informs business decisions. According to a report by Forrester, "Time and money spent on data and analytics enablement, from data democratization to embedded analytics, is wasted when work is not connected to business decisions."[36]

The second problem with data relates to consistency. Different parts of the organization may use tools that define key terms differently. The word "customer" may mean one thing to finance, another thing to customer service, and yet another to sales or marketing. Words like "site visit" and "conversion" also vary between tools. If you define metrics based on data from different sources, take care not to compare across tools—at least without checking such definitions and calculations for consistency.

Even if there is consistent data, you must use caution in how you position it. When assessing directions to improve products, any data the team has agreed to use is fair game. But that same data may be politically dangerous when working with senior managers. Try to keep management focused on longer time frames and goals that are closer to corporate priorities, because if your senior VP is staring at data dashboards and noticing that needles aren't moving from day to day or week to week, then you've set expectations poorly, and your project may end up in danger.

An even bigger problem than data consistency is alignment around goals. Feedback loops can only work if everyone buys in up front that the team will use (admittedly imperfect) measurement tools and address the problems they point to, regardless of any preconceived notions. We recommend having an open conversation among your leadership team on how statistically viable or "perfect" data must be to serve as the basis for a decision on any given initiative. For some projects, directional data may suffice, while others require more statistical rigor or confidence.

HOW DATA CAN BECOME A LEADING INDICATOR

The advantage of feedback loops is that they provide an unbiased test of what's working, what's not, and what must change next. When you've got feedback like that, you can make improvements at a rapid pace. And that's how to keep your organization as responsive as a highly tuned race car.

When you become adept enough with this sort of feedback, you begin to develop the capability to develop predictive insights from data. You can see where the users and the market are going and shift the product to prepare. Using pattern recognition to predict what user reaction and feedback will be before it arrives is the next level of sophistication.

Feedback loops then evolve from trailing indicators to leading indicators. And all of that is possible because your teams developed the skill to embed feedback loops in their work.

Part IV

TECHNOLOGY AND THE FUTURE

Chapter 10

ALIGNING TECHNOLOGY WITH VALUE

Remember the credit union from chapter 3? As it turns out, the customer-centric actions it took on dispute resolution and credit card approvals were not the only ways it embraced modernized technology to improve its responsiveness.

The credit union turned next to its consumer loans—with a total value of $40 billion. Was there a way to streamline the speed with which it could turn around loan requests?

The challenge here was one that many organizations face: a slow and obsolescing set of legacy technology platforms that have accumulated technical debt—that is, a failure to keep up with and modernize key systems. Since those systems often contain key data that's essential for processes like loan origination, they become an obstacle to the goal of making the enterprise more responsive.

The essential first step was to assess the problem with the loan origination application. A technical assessment revealed problems stemming from a legacy system. These problems included backlogs for requested fixes that slowed even the simplest changes and improvements, a shrinking pool of resources to support the application, and missed opportunities on other projects because of the expanding demands created by the legacy application. Projected improvements frequently were months late and ran over budget by $1 million or more. The system wasn't easily accessible to other applications through APIs, and additional requests to connect to it bogged things down further since its applications interfaces weren't designed to scale up. As a result, as the systems slowed, employees struggled to serve customers quickly. The credit union's loan capabilities weren't competitive with next-generation financial tech companies like Rocket Mortgage, and the credit union's loan department had sunk into a culture of paralysis and denial about its challenges.

Building Agile methodology processes on top of this legacy framework was not going to be enough. It was time to rethink the base technology.

We worked with the credit union's technology management team to build a business case for a new platform. After conducting a series of interviews internally, we documented the relationships among applications and the challenges that the technical debt was causing. A rigorous analysis of competitors' offerings added further fuel to the case to revamp the system. This analysis, along with a comparison of the capabilities of potential new replacements for the loan-origination systems, helped enable the team to make an informed, data-driven decision to modernize the entire platform.

The new platform would have the capabilities needed for a modern, responsive set of applications. It would be omnichannel—that is, available with interfaces for internal employee access, access through websites, and visibility through mobile and other modern application modalities. The new solution would be scalable for new interfaces and would support growth. Processing and funding times would be reduced to minutes. Going forward, not only do we expect significant improvements in the ability to speed loan-origination decisions and customer experience, but the more responsive system will likely also improve the morale and culture of the loan department, bringing it in line with the other responsive attributes of the credit union overall.

RESPONSIVE ENTERPRISES ARE BUILT ON TECHNOLOGY—BUT THE IT DEPARTMENT IS RARELY RESPONSIVE

No matter what kind of business you are in, technology is always intimately involved in the change to become more responsive. Every element of the responsive enterprise—customer centricity, operational excellence, and enterprise agility—relies on a stable foundation of technology.

Whose job is it to maintain and improve that technology? Often, the IT department. In the Forrester Consulting survey of business decision-makers throughout the enterprise, 49% said IT is the group responsible for "adjusting our operations to accommodate changes in our business environment"—more than product, marketing, and eBusiness groups.

And therein lies a real challenge for responsiveness: the relationships of IT departments and the rest of the business. Traditionally, IT has been where technology lived—and that meant technology infrastructure, big systems of record like customer databases and inventory systems, and development teams. But IT has a (frequently) well-earned reputation for being *un*responsive. IT departments are chronically underfunded because they tend to live far from the parts of the organization where revenue is generated. They get blamed for failures and security issues, so they're inherently risk-averse. If technology moves slowly, how can a responsive enterprise be built from technology?

Our VP of technology advisory, Jon Tolmach, offers a solution: Align technology investments with value. The parts of the company that depend on these core technologies must take charge of—and fund—the base-level technologies they depend on. This means that the responsibility for many core applications will move from IT into marketing, sales, customer service, or product development. They will still use IT resources, but those resources will work side by side with the value-creating elements of the business. Once again, a cross-functional team of IT and business unit staff becomes the driving force for improvements to these technology components.

Having groups outside of IT take much of the responsibility for technology applications seems at first glance like a radical idea, but it is already happening. Marketing departments have technically skilled teams running complex and essential marketing technology suites based on applications like Salesforce or Adobe's Marketing Cloud, along with collections of allied tools and add-ons. In the past, technologies hatched and nurtured outside of IT were often referred to, in a disparaging tone, as "shadow IT" projects. But shadow IT is no longer in the shadows, and it's long past time to give these technology efforts formal recognition. To the extent that they create value for the enterprise, these technology efforts should be served through a more conscious alignment of IT (resources, capabilities, standards, architectures) to the business to execute together; simply "recentralizing" them back into IT is not the way to keep the value flowing responsively.

In theory, technology can solve nearly any problem. But in any given enterprise, technology cannot solve all the problems at once. Technology investments are expensive. The way to prioritize them is to identify where they contribute to value, and that includes contributions made by the legacy systems and infrastructure that ultimately power the value-generating portions of the enterprise. That is the business logic behind a transformation that aligns technology systems and investments with the value they create.

The idea of moving sole responsibility for major systems out of IT and turning it over to a cross-functional team seems shocking. So let's take a closer look at IT attitudes to see why it might be necessary.

IT DECISION-MAKERS KNOW THERE IS A PROBLEM

In 2023, Randstad surveyed more than 750 IT decision-makers in the US and Canada.[37] What the survey revealed about IT departments was troubling for business responsiveness.

The decision-makers in this survey know they occupy a pivotal role. Nine in ten of them believe that technology is key to their company heading in the right direction, and a similar number feel that continuous improvement of their IT infrastructure is crucial to their ability to succeed as an organization.

That said, half of the CIOs in the survey are either not satisfied with the direction technology is taking their business or doubt their key initiatives will be successful in the next five years. Moreover, three out of four associate this doubt with poor system performance, outdated technology, or missing technology.

Out-of-date technology is an endemic problem. A troubling 41% of technology decision-makers in the survey reported that they've had low success in modernizing the organization's technology to meet business needs. Moving forward, one in three lacked confidence in their organization's ability to deliver on key initiatives and to modernize technology over the next five years.

Underfunding technology is chronic. And it's getting worse; 44% of respondents to the survey said it's an issue that's likely to become more acute in the current economic climate.

The chasm between IT and the business exacerbates the problems. Four in ten IT decision-makers have low involvement in wider strategy beyond their own department.

This is why it's time to reconsider where responsibility for base technologies—and their budgets—live in the organization.

ALIGNING TECHNOLOGY WITH VALUE CAN BREAK DOWN SILOS

It might seem counterintuitive that having departments take responsibility for their own technology infrastructure could break down counterproductive silos. Surely a central technology function acquiring and maintaining tech for other parts of the business would be better at ensuring connections.

In reality, though, this isn't what happens. Organizationally, groups consistently focus on their own needs. This means IT must focus on reducing risk and improving security, rather than growth. And other functions focus on the bits of technology they need—and the data they produce—to the detriment of open collaboration.

But breaking down silos is essential to the operation of the responsive enterprise. Customer centricity, operational excellence, and enterprise agility all move forward with the efforts of cross-functional teams. Those teams need a responsive base of technology to build on. That requires technology investments that continue to be aligned with where the organization is creating value.

Breaking down silos means more than just changing who's responsible for key technologies. That shift must be accompanied by cultural change. Workers across departments must spend more time collaborating on systems like Slack or Microsoft Teams. Communication strategist Melissa Agnes recommends company-wide messaging efforts and training to focus workers on value, rather than more limited departmental goals.[38] Narrow, department-focused incentives need to yield to compensation based on broader, cross-departmental successes.

To position technology cross-functionally, organizations must acquire new attitudes toward both data and applications architecture.

DATA DEMOCRATIZATION MUST PROVIDE ACTIONABLE INFORMATION, NOT JUST ACCESS

It's impossible for parts of a company to move forward responsively if data is trapped in silos. Data democratization provides the fuel that cross-functional teams need to do their work. We referred to data democratization in the previous chapter as an essential part of the data need for feedback loops. But the need goes further: organizations must weave data democratization into their overall philosophy of development.

As Des Cahill, a group vice president in marketing at Oracle, points out, "The companies that invested in the democratization of their data were the ones to weather the pandemic and accelerate out of it." Abishek Viswanathan, a former group product director at Qualtrics, recommends that companies "focus on the right outcomes and having the right data to support it. Make sure that your data is embedded in all the tools your employees are using every day, and then bring in the right context."[39]

Access by itself is insufficient. It's necessary to build tools that bring that data in actionable form to the teams that need it, when they need it. This means building a 360-degree view of the customer accessible with information from customer-facing applications in sales and marketing, as well as data from billing and finance—and making that view accessible to everyone. To be actionable, such a view requires data visualization tools that assemble intelligence from different sources, enabling data-based decisions to prioritize features and long-term investment. Analytics—including both diagnostic tools like customer journey analytics and applications that incorporate predictive analytics—are possible only with solid and open data connections.

WHEN TECHNOLOGY IS DISTRIBUTED, MICROSERVICES BECOME ESSENTIAL

Throughout this book, we've drawn a portrait of Agile groups and other innovators creating and constantly improving applications. The teams working on those improvements are typically small and cross-functional. But they can only do their work if they have regular dependable interfaces to major legacy systems.

Consider what happens when a new technology channel emerges—as mobile apps did in the mid-2010s, smart speakers did in the late 2010s, and generative AI based on large language models is doing now. Enterprises hoping to deliver improved customer experiences in those technology channels need rapid and dependable access to the systems that the organization runs on. Mobile apps for airlines need access to reservation systems. Interactive media streaming services need connections to digitized content and customer systems. AI-based financial prediction systems need real-time access to news feeds and historical trends data.

The ideal architecture for such connections is microservices: packaged program interfaces that deliver dependable, instant connections to underlying databases and transactions. A microservice might make it possible for a mobile app to enable a stock purchase, a smart speaker to access a Spotify playlist, or a retailer to send a text message when a product's price drops. Organizations must engineer such services to be independently deployable, robustly dependable, and secure. Crucially, these services should also be independent of the channels in which they operate. If a microservice at a travel company enables a consumer to check on the status of a flight, that same microservice should be useful regardless of whether that request is coming from a website, a mobile app, a smart speaker, a text-based chat, or some not yet fully imagined modality like virtual reality.

One key benefit of microservices is that they can be scaled up more easily, independently of each other. This is smart engineering that supports new connections and new applications, because those new connections often generate massive or unpredictable surges in loads. Consider what happens to a travel company's reservation and rescheduling microservices when snowstorms shut down a string of Midwest airports or the loads that a stock-trading microservice might need to withstand in the midst of a rapidly diving stock market.

These demands are the reason that investments in technology must be aligned with value. If an organization has not engineered its legacy systems in such a way that they're accessible to microservices, then sales, marketing, service, or product development functions must invest to upgrade them. If they're failing under a load, that's usually a sign of a missed opportunity. If technical debt is crippling them, it may be time to invest in modernizing. In this new alignment, there are more productive ways to create change than screaming at a beleaguered IT department; revenue-generating portions of the business can prioritize the improvements and the costs—and the promise of value—associated with them.

These demands will inevitably drive applications in a modern direction. Homegrown, difficult-to-maintain solutions will be replaced by COTS (customized off-the-shelf) applications supported by major technology vendors because only such vendor-based solutions will stay up to date with changes in technology. Such solutions will be multi-tenant and cloud-based with modern APIs. They'll be at the center of an ecosystem of associated plug-ins and enhancements. Those up-to-date vendor applications aren't usually the cheapest solutions, but over the long run, they represent an investment in the ease of updating and connecting to all the groups at the organization that need them.

Many of these legacy systems will be essential to more than one value-generating group. If one function takes over responsibility for an application, it must also be responsible for maintaining the systems and modernizing the connections for groups across the enterprise. In the end, much of the value is likely to come from silo-busting cross-functional teams. So this change isn't just about shifting responsibility, it's about maintaining those legacy systems and interfaces in ways that are commensurate with value that could come from anywhere in the enterprise.

IT BECOMES A VALUE CREATOR AS A CENTER OF EXCELLENCE

Are we to hollow out all the IT departments as we remove responsibility for all the applications to more directly value-creating parts of the business? What's left for IT to do?

Only the two most important jobs the enterprise needs.

First, of course, is infrastructure. The workers still need access to devices, servers, corporate systems, and all the rest of the infrastructure it takes to keep the business running. If the machines stop working— or if they become insecure and get hacked—then the value creation becomes irrelevant.

But the second essential job is to function as a technology center of excellence.

IT will maintain the organization's operating model and the data models associated with it. This is the realm of enterprise architecture, the conceptual blueprint for legacy applications and processes, as well as more modern modifications to them. As AI becomes more prevalent, enterprise architecture can become even more detailed. AI expert Seth Earley, author of *The AI-Powered Enterprise,* makes the point that a modern organization should be maintaining an ontology—a complete model of the data and data flows associated with all the key technologies in the enterprise. IT is where this ontology lives.

In addition to maintaining the enterprise architecture, IT becomes a trusted advisor for functions and departments deploying technology. No organization should make a multimillion-dollar investment in tech without consulting with those in the organization who've made such investments before. In its new role, IT can also drive standardization and consistency for technology across the enterprise.

And as organizations roll out new improvements to technology, the IT group may become the home of a center of excellence for Agile methodologies, or for modern development methodologies like DevOps, a set of tools that enable rapid deployment and automated testing.

In short, IT becomes the trusted advisor for best practices on technology rollouts and improvements.

This organizational model—in which technology systems and investments align with the groups creating value, and best practices and expertise are centralized in IT—is one that will enable organizations to move quickly and responsively, but also safely and efficiently. And that's crucial, because technology has become so central to organizations' ability to compete.

Chapter 11

RESPONSIVE ENTERPRISES WILL RULE THE FUTURE

We've now described all the elements of a responsive enterprise. But does it truly matter? Are responsive enterprises actually more successful?

Throughout this book, we have been describing the study of 418 North American digital strategy decision-makers we commissioned Forrester Consulting to do on our behalf. The study included scoring responses to questions regarding customer centricity, operational effectiveness, and agility. These responses enabled us to divide all the respondents into three categories based on an overall responsiveness maturity score. We used this to compare the most responsive 15% (identified in the study as "high maturity") to the least responsive 15% (identified as "low maturity").

Surprisingly, the high-maturity firms were more likely to be larger, with revenues of $1 billion or more. And they were more concentrated in financial services and retail.

Naturally, the most responsive firms were more likely to prioritize customer centricity, operational effectiveness, and agility in their decisions than the low-maturity firms. In fact, it was the focus on *all three* of these areas that set the most responsive firms apart. That commitment extended beyond prioritization to investment: The most responsive firms were twice as likely to be investing in responsive capabilities for their companies (see table 11-1). And these investments paid off with customers: 94% of the executives in the most responsive companies consistently reported that they met or exceeded customer expectations, while only 73% of those in the least responsive companies did.

	HIGH MATURITY (on scale of responsiveness)	LOW MATURITY (on scale of responsiveness)
More likely larger firms ($1B+)	45%	33%
More likely to be in financial services	23%	8%
More likely to be in retail	17%	3%
More likely to prioritize customer centricity	97%	80%
More likely to prioritize operational effectiveness	97%	69%
More likely to prioritize agility	89%	61%
More likely to invest in responsive capabilities	49%	25%
Consistently meet/exceed customer expectations	94%	73%

Table 11-1. Comparison of high- and low-maturity firms on a responsiveness scale.
Source: A commissioned study conducted by Forrester Consulting on behalf of Celerity, November 2021. Base: 418 North American digital strategy decision-makers.

But what truly stood out from this research were the dramatic differences in the financial performance of the companies whose responsiveness rated them as high maturity. Consistently, the most responsive companies were more likely to have increased revenue, profit, share price, market valuation, and earnings per share over the past five years (see figure 11-1).

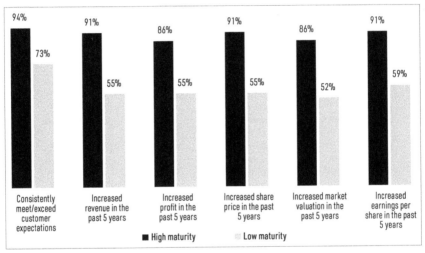

Figure 11-1. Responsive companies are more profitable.
Source: A commissioned study conducted by Forrester Consulting on behalf of Celerity, November 2021. Base: 418 North American digital strategy decision-makers.

Further investigation reveals more dimensions to the superior performance of the most responsive companies. More responsive companies are dramatically more successful at achieving their key business goals. They are five times as likely to overperform against quickly responding to changing customer and market needs, twice as likely to overperform on meeting customer demand and expectations, and four times more successful at finding partners who can support their customer-oriented strategy.

This reflects a deliberate choice of company strategy: Responsive firms were also more likely to say that the three responsiveness qualities play an important or mission-critical role in their success. Highly responsive firms are also twice as likely as those less responsive to highlight the importance of customer experience design and innovation, as well as enterprise architecture and technology modernization.

Executives in the study highlighted the importance of responsiveness. As an IT leader in retail remarked, "Look, if we don't prioritize [responsiveness], then our competition will. With how retail is, if you're not on top of changes in your environment, then you're putting yourself in a position where your customer can easily choose to go somewhere else."

Agility and responsiveness are top of mind for these decision-makers. As an IT executive in financial services shared, "Our strategies are never set in stone, really. They're reviewed on an ongoing basis, usually quarterly—are we achieving what we expected? And then things are funded quarterly based on those reviews—how are you progressing in terms of your vision? It's also about getting away from a waterfall approach where someone spends a year in a room to develop a strategy and do their part, then pass it off to another year's worth of implementation. Now we get our architects and our builders together in the room and let them work in a synchronized way."

If you're interested in resources regarding these concepts, go to our book site at responsiveenterprise.com. You can also download a copy of the white paper that Forrester Consulting created from the data in the study and access links to more case studies on enterprises that made gains by adopting responsive enterprise principles and practices.

HOW RESPONSIVE ENTERPRISES WILL INFLUENCE THE FUTURE

As we described in chapter 1, we're in a period of rapid change that challenges businesses as never before—from pandemic disruptions to political unrest to a war in Europe to stubborn inflation. Industry by industry, technology is disrupting established companies from retail to autos to media. Artificial intelligence, in the form of large language models, threatens to transform or displace every job category. As Bill Gates wrote:[40]

> The development of AI is as fundamental as the creation of the microprocessor, the personal computer, the Internet, and the mobile phone. It will change the way people work, learn, travel, get health care, and communicate with each other. Entire industries will reorient around it. Businesses will distinguish themselves by how well they use it.

Among other industries, the energy business may be in for a big change. As an article in the *New York Times* stated after a recent breakthrough, "If fusion can be deployed on a large scale, it would offer an energy source devoid of the pollution and greenhouse gases caused by the burning of fossil fuels and the dangerous long-lived radioactive waste created by current nuclear power plants, which use the splitting of uranium to produce energy."[41]

We cannot predict what major shifts are just over the horizon. In the face of profound and pervasive change, responsiveness is imperative. It's the one skill that enables everything else an enterprise does to continue to create value.

We've seen how customer centricity, operational excellence, and enterprise agility will fuel that responsiveness. Companies that embrace those principles will learn not just what to do, but also how to act in the face of change. They will continually think strategically while making constant tactical adjustments.

Success will come from a focus on innovations both large and small. Day-to-day, responsive companies will make continual shifts and adjustments, reacting more quickly and effectively and making steady gains against slower-moving competitors. But those same innovative and responsive instincts will prepare enterprises for what are likely to be more frequent exposures to existential crises.

Ironically, crises create opportunity. As Rahm Emanuel said when he was chief of staff to President Barack Obama, "You never want a serious crisis to go to waste. And what I mean by that is an opportunity to do things that you think you could not do before."

These crises will show us what companies are made of.

Some will transform themselves. Consider Microsoft, which for decades was faced with a steady onslaught of competitive pressure as it attempted to preserve its operating system from inroads by Apple and its applications from competition from Google. As Behnam Tabrizi wrote in *Harvard Business Review* in 2023, "For years now, observers of tech have written off Microsoft as a 20th-century phenomenon, fat and happy from its Windows monopoly. The tech giant hadn't had a break-through innovation in decades. It was rich enough to be a fast follower, but too big and bureaucratic to lead in any market."[42]

But under CEO Satya Nadella, Microsoft began to listen and behave in a more agile way. As Tabrizi wrote, "Microsoft's cultural transformation involved . . . an obsession with customers. . . . Rather than go by sales, a lagging indicator in fast-moving [software] markets, or even what customers were saying, Nadella had product developers focus on what people were actually using. They set up dashboards to see usage over the previous month, to get an up-to-date sense of the market." Such dashboards would enable them, not just to see what was happening, but also to identify trends through predictive analytics. Crucially, the company embraced agility, reducing hierarchies and relaxing institutional controls and rigid approval rules to allow engineers to innovate, rather than wrestle with bureaucracy.

Microsoft surprisingly began to embrace the market for development tools for competing operating systems like Linux and Apple's iOS. And in early 2023, Microsoft opportunistically pounced, enhancing its Bing search tool and its productivity applications like Word, Excel, and PowerPoint with dramatic new capabilities from an AI large language model, leaving Google flat-footed.

But for every Microsoft, there is an enterprise that focuses all its energy on just withstanding a crisis, rather than embracing the opportunity for change, and fails. Take Sears, which acquired Lands' End to embrace online sales, but then withered amid competition from more innovative retailers like Walmart and Amazon. With thousands of locations, RadioShack attempted to reinvent itself as a reseller of satellite TV and mobile service, but failed to change its basic model and imploded.

Most enterprises will not vaporize as Blockbuster, Polaroid, Circuit City, Borders, Ringling Brothers, A&P, Zenith, Oldsmobile, and Toys "R" Us did. Even so, they're more likely to expend all their energy attempting to defend their existing models rather than to transform in response to change. Exhausted by that effort, they'll end up second-tier players in markets they used to dominate, with reduced profitability and market share. If these companies don't learn to embrace change in the face of the crises that face them, as Microsoft did, then they've wasted the opportunity to build responsiveness and resilience into their culture and methods. Thus begins the race to the bottom.

LEGACY INFRASTRUCTURE WILL HOLD COMPANIES BACK

At the heart of many companies hoping to change is an inflexible, outmoded, hard-to-optimize lump of core technology. We're talking bank systems still coded in COBOL, mainframe inventory systems, and crucial but outmoded information infrastructure holding companies back like a boat anchor.

These problems matter. In his book about artificial intelligence, *The Age of Intent,* PV Kannan, the CEO of the innovative customer service and chatbot company [24]7.ai, tells of a large online retailer that was hoping to use AI to modernize its system for support requests from merchant partners.[43] The AI would need to be connected to an essential code module within the company called the "decisioning engine" that looked at the characteristics of the account requesting a change and returned a decision about what to do. The decisioning engine was quite consistent: 95% of the time, it returned the answer, "Transfer to [human] agent." It should have been called an "indecisioning engine."

The project leader for the AI project identified the source of the problem and pleaded with four different executives at the company who shared responsibility for the decisioning engine, hoping to get permission to modernize it. But as Kannan relates, "Over time, the code in the decisioning engine had become so intricate and interdependent that everyone was afraid to make the slightest change. It remained a glowing, active component at the heart of the system, completely opaque and impervious to improvement."

This is what technical debt in legacy systems looks like: essential technology that resists modernization. Such systems block efforts to be responsive.

As we described in the previous chapter, the ultimate solution here is to move responsibility for these systems into the parts of the company that generate value—so that such groups can make the necessary investments to modernize what's holding them back. But we acknowledge that many companies will not have the boldness to accept our advice.

Regardless of how responsive they hope to be, their technology will slow them down.

They'll suffer twice.

First, their competitors will be able to innovate while they're hamstrung by the speed of their core systems, so they'll face constant attrition of customers to competitors, whether that competition comes from disruptive start-ups or established players who've successfully become more responsive.

Second, when whatever unexpected crisis arrives to challenge their company—driven by interrupted supply chains, government regulation roiled by political turmoil, rapid AI-based technology shifts, bank failures, or the next pandemic—they'll be powerless to respond because their systems will keep clanking away at the same slow and deadly pace.

A character in Ernest Hemingway's novel *The Sun Also Rises* described how he went bankrupt: "Two ways. Gradually and then suddenly." Similarly, these companies held back by their systems will lose share and relevance, first steadily and then abruptly.

Companies that fail to invest to modernize core systems will face steady profit and market pressure. The responsive companies that have made the investment will gain at their expense.

Eventually, inevitably, the responsive enterprises will acquire the laggards' companies. They'll keep their valuable assets like products, contracts, customer bases, and data, even as they dump their legacy systems by the side of the road.

RESPONSIVENESS WILL ELEVATE THE MOST INSPIRED FUTURE LEADERS

Where will the brightest, most creative professionals end up? At the responsive companies.

Consider what it's like for a worker. At a responsive company, you work for a common goal across functions. The challenge is different from day to day because you'll be iterating your efforts based on a changing perception of customer needs. As your industry and your company's position within it change, your work will change.

In other words, it will be exciting and challenging—and it will be clear every day that you are making a difference.

There is room in this environment for all sorts of bright people. That includes creative problem solvers, meticulous detail-oriented people, effective communicators and collaborators, and inspirational leaders.

And, as we described at the start of this chapter, in responsive companies there is a high likelihood of growth and profit, which create both career and financial opportunities for workers.

People who are satisfied with the steady state, with doing the same thing over and over again, are more likely to stay with companies where change moves slowly. The ambitious, adventurous ones will be more likely to move. As a result, we expect a steady shift of talent from less responsive to more responsive companies.

We are in the midst of a generational shift in leadership. The next generation of corporate leaders will be professionals raised in a world of evolving technology, but matured by the global upheavals of the twenty-first century: the war on terror, the Great Recession, the polarized politics, and the COVID-19 pandemic. Workers who have seen Tesla's value exceed Mercedes-Benz's, Netflix dominate Hollywood, Amazon bedevil Best Buy, and Apple best HP are better prepared to help their organizations to adapt to a world of constantly shifting technology-fueled consumer demands.

TAKE HEART AND LEAD

There are a thousand details that go into what it takes to embrace the principles of the responsive enterprise. Managers and business researchers will be studying this trend for decades. But at its heart, the concept of responsiveness is as much an attitude as it is a set of practices.

That attitude commits to addressing the ever-changing nature of customer needs, to moving efficiently to deliver on those needs, and to embracing agility as a keystone cultural value.

Disruption is terrifying to managers raised on a diet of steady-state strategy. But it's exhilarating to the professionals in a responsive enterprise. They recognize that while comfort is never a good sign, as long as employees are empowered to make decisions in an environment that fosters psychological safety and know they won't get fired if and when they fail, they have the confidence to take some calculated risks and try new things. In such organizations, movement must not just be constant, but also move in a constantly adjusting, customer-centric direction.

The true vision here is that customer centricity, operational excellence, and enterprise agility are necessary, but not fully sufficient for success. Exposing value, embracing systems thinking, empowering teams, and embedding feedback loops are steps along the way. They train us to think of ourselves and our organization as responsive.

Much of what is important to enterprises is changing and will continue to change. How we create applications will change. So will how we collaborate and how we communicate with each other. What we deliver will be different in the future from what it has been in the past. The ways we understand customers will change, and the needs and desires of those customers will be continually shifting.

To you, the executive in a responsive enterprise, these constant changes signal opportunity. You will have the tools and the capability to move faster and more effectively to thrive on change.

We know you can do this. It will be a more varied and less complacent workplace, but it will never be boring. It's the gateway to a universe of potential opportunities.

The future belongs to the responsive. The time to start thinking differently is now.

ACKNOWLEDGMENTS

We are deeply grateful to the many individuals, team members, and clients who have made this book possible. First and foremost, we want to acknowledge Ken Quaglio and the 2018 Celerity leadership team for originating the idea of the responsive enterprise in a conference room at the Inn at Willow Grove. Without their brilliant vision and commitment, this book would not exist.

We would also like to express our appreciation to Joe Benvenuto, Graeme Booth, Kim Carter, Jessica Dunn, Kathy Hebert, Aaron Kennelly, Ron Millanti, David Nickelson, Anne Parmer, Rick Schantz, Rebecca Sweda, and Jon Tolmach for their invaluable contributions to refining the idea and operationalizing the responsive enterprise for countless clients. Their expertise and dedication have been essential in shaping the ideas and concepts presented in this book.

We are also grateful to Rob Ganjon, JT Scott, and Melissa Young for the unique perspectives they contributed to the narrative of this book.

Their insights and experiences have enriched the content and provided additional depth and context to the ideas presented.

Finally, we would like to extend a heartfelt thanks to all the people who have supported us throughout the writing process, including Josh Bernoff; our family, friends, colleagues; and the team at our publisher, Ideapress. The encouragement and feedback has been invaluable, and we are truly thankful for their unwavering support of our work.

ABOUT THE AUTHORS

CURT SCHWAB

With more than twenty-five years of leadership and consulting experience focused on digital transformation, Curt Schwab has played a pivotal role in guiding Fortune 100 companies, small and medium businesses, and government agencies through rapid change. Curt is a lifelong learner and enjoys exploring the intersection of data, technology, AI, and their collective impact on business results.

Curt served as president and chief client officer at the business and technology consulting firm, Celerity, a wholly owned operating company of Randstad. Over a period of three years, Curt rebuilt the executive team, instilled a high-performance culture, and repositioned the company's service offerings to align with market demand. These efforts transformed a five-year declining business into two consecutive years of double-digit top-line growth and margin expansion. He also served on the Randstad Executive Leadership Team, where he played a central role in the consolidation of approximately fifteen operating companies to form a $5 billion global technology company, Randstad Global Technologies Group.

Prior to joining Celerity, Curt founded and served as CEO of the digital consulting firm Blue Water, a technology transformation leader helping clients such as Audi, L3Harris, Marriott, and Capital One. He successfully orchestrated the firm's acquisition in 2019. Curt was also the CEO, and later transitioned to the chairman role, of leading SaaS software provider Waterfall Software. Over the course of his career, Curt has founded, exponentially grown, and successfully exited numerous businesses. This entrepreneurial spirit combined with a deep understanding of business fundamentals translates into high-value relationships that are based on results.

Curt graduated from the Business Analytics Program at The Wharton School and has a BA from the University of Colorado, Boulder. He is a member of the invite-only CEO community Mindshare; the Customer Experience Professionals Association (CXPA); and the George Washington University Customer Experience Advisory Board. Curt is a frequent speaker at conferences and industry events and is actively involved in promoting the importance of data science, machine learning, and artificial intelligence for younger generations through high school and university programs.

Curt resides in Annapolis, Maryland, with his wife, two teenage sons, and his Bernese Mountain dog. Contact him at curt@curtschwab.com.

KATIE MARKWELL

Katie Markwell leads the business and technology consulting group at Randstad Digital (formerly Celerity) and serves as the senior vice president of Advisory Services. She is responsible for all aspects of client service and global delivery for its advisory offerings and verticals. With a career spanning eighteen years, her expertise lies in service excellence across business and technology domains, including customer experience, agile delivery, and operational transformation. She helps organizations and their leaders drive clarity, respond to change, and improve overall performance.

Katie has provided strategic guidance to private and nonprofit organizations of various sizes and industries, both as an in-house leader and as a consulting partner. Under Katie's leadership, Celerity's team has achieved world-class Net Promoter Scores, innovation awards, and client appreciation. Prior to her current position, Katie had roles of increasing responsibility in sales research, branding and advertising, digital innovation, and customer experience. She is an active member of the Washington, DC, chapter of Chief, a private network designed for senior women leaders to cross-pollinate ideas across industries and effect change from the top down. She is a graduate of Randstad's Senior Executive Program for high-performing executive leaders.

Katie earned her bachelor of arts in English from Wake Forest University and a master of arts in sociolinguistics from Georgetown University. Katie currently resides in Falls Church, Virginia, with her husband and their two Lakeland Terriers.

ENDNOTES

1   "Future of Jobs Report 2023," World Economic Forum, May 2023, https://www3.weforum.org/docs/WEF_Future_of_Jobs_2023.pdf.

2   "Recession and Automation Changes Our Future of Work, but There Are Jobs Coming, Report Says," news release, World Economic Forum, October 20, 2020, https://www.weforum.org/press/2020/10/recession-and-automation-changes-our-future-of-work-but-there-are-jobs-coming-report-says-52c5162fce/.

3   "When Disruption Reigns, Let Your Customers Show You the Way," a commissioned study conducted by Forrester Consulting on behalf of Celerity, March 2022.

4   Source: "Resilience 2022: Interos Annual Global Supply Chain Report," May 11, 2022, https://www.interos.ai/resources/global-supply-chain-report/.

5   We follow the industry practice of capitalizing Agile when it refers to the software development methodology, but not capitalizing it in reference to the more general quality of agility in enterprises.

6   "ACSI Scores as Financial Indicators," ACSI, 2022. ACSI® is a registered trademark of the American Customer Satisfaction Index, https://www.theacsi.org/the-acsi-difference/acsi-scores-as-financial-indicators/.

7   Chris Hurn, "Stuffed Giraffe Shows What Customer Service Is All About," *HuffPost*, May 17, 2012, https://www.huffpost.com/entry/stuffed-giraffe-shows-wha_b_1524038.

8   This framework was originally developed by the design firm IDEO, https://www.ideou.com/blogs/inspiration/how-to-prototype-a-new-business.

9   Rikke Friis Dam and Teo Yu Siang, "The History of Design Thinking," Interaction Design Foundation, June 2022, https://www.interaction-design.org/literature/article/design-thinking-get-a-quick-overview-of-the-history.

10 "What is Design Thinking," IDEO U, https://www.ideou.com/blogs/inspiration/what-is-design-thinking.

11 Raffaella Sadun, Nicholas Bloom, and John Van Reenen, "Why Do We Undervalue Competent Management?," *Harvard Business Review*, September–October 2017, https://hbr.org/2017/09/why-do-we-undervalue-competent-management.

12 SEAL is a service mark of Celerity.

13 Seth Earley, "There's No AI without IA," *IEEE Xplore*, May–June 2016, https://ieeexplore.ieee.org/document/747858.1.

14 Clayton M. Christensen, Richard Alton, Curtis Rising, and Andrew Waldeck, "The Big Idea: The New M&A Playbook," *Harvard Business Review,* March 2011, https://hbr.org/2011/03/the-big-idea-the-new-ma-playbook.

15 Matt Ashare, "A Waterfall Regress: Agile Momentum Limited by Issues of Scale," *CIO Dive*, May 3, 2022, https://www.ciodive.com/news/waterfall-regress-agile-momentum-forrester/623135/.

16 "State of Agile Report," Digital.ai, https://digital.ai/resource-center/analyst-reports/state-of-agile-report/.

17 "Gartner Glossary," Gartner, https://www.gartner.com/en/information-technology/glossary/product-digital-business.

18 Michele Parmelee, "The Deloitte Global 2021 Millennial and Gen Z Survey: Highlights," Deloitte, June 15, 2021, https://www.deloitte.com/global/en/our-thinking/insights/topics/talent/deloitte-millennial-survey-2021.html.

19 Martin Reeves, Lars Fæste, Kevin Whitaker, and Fabien Hassan, "The Truth about Corporate Transformation," *MIT Sloan Management Review*, January 31, 2018, https://sloanreview.mit.edu/article/the-truth-about-corporate-transformation/.

20 Paul A. Argenti, Jenifer Berman, Ryan Calsbeek, and Andrew Whitehouse, "The Secret Behind Successful Corporate Transformations," *Harvard Business Review*, September 14, 2021, https://hbr.org/2021/09/the-secret-behind-successful-corporate-transformations.

21 Jurica Novak and Tim Dickson, "Leading a Corporate Transformation," *McKinsey Quarterly*, January 23, 2017, https://www.mckinsey.com/capabilities/people-and-organizational-performance/our-insights/leading-a-corporate-transformation.

22 "Workmonitor 2023," Randstad, https://workforceinsights.randstad.com/workmonitor-2023.

23 "Talent Trends 2023," Randstad Enterprise, https://www.randstadsourceright.com/talent-trends/.

24 Daniel Kim, "Introduction to Systems Thinking," *The Systems Thinker*, https://thesystemsthinker.com/introduction-to-systems-thinking/.

25 Nick Sonnenberg, "How Jeff Bezos Used the 2-Pizza Rule to Put an End to Useless Meetings at Amazon," *Inc.*, October 26, 2022, https://www.inc.com/nicholas-sonnenberg/jeff-bezos-2-pizza-rule-meetings-at-amazon.html.

26 Chris DeBrusk, "Get Things Done with Smaller Teams," *MIT Sloan Management Review*, September 7, 2018, https://sloanreview.mit.edu/article/get-things-done-with-smaller-teams/.

27 Marty Kagan with Chris Jones, *Empowered: Ordinary People, Extraordinary Products* (Wiley, 2021), p. 78.

28 Ibid., p. 9.

29 "Mercenaries vs. Missionaries: John Doerr Sees Two Kinds of Internet Entrepreneurs," *Knowledge at Wharton*, April 13, 2000, https://knowledge.wharton.upenn.edu/article/mercenaries-vs-missionaries-john-doerr-sees-two-kinds-of-internet-entrepreneurs/.

30 Natalia M. Lorinkova, Matthew J. Pearsall, and Henry P. Sims Jr, "Examining the Differential Longitudinal Performance of Directive versus Empowering Leadership in Teams," *Academy of Management Journal* 56, No. 2, May 7, 2012, https://journals.aom.org/doi/10.5465/amj.2011.0132.

31 Vanessa Urch Druskat and Jane V. Wheeler, "How to Lead a Self-Managing Team," *MIT Sloan Management Review,* July 15, 2004, https://sloanreview.mit.edu/article/how-to-lead-a-selfmanaging-team/.

32 Judith Stein, "Using the Stages of Team Development," *MIT Human Resources,* https://hr.mit.edu/learning-topics/teams/articles/stages-development. Original article: B. W. Tuckman, "Developmental Sequence in Small Groups," *Psychology Bulletin,* June 1965, https://pubmed.ncbi.nlm.nih.gov/14314073/.

33 Josh Bernoff and Ted Schadler, *Empowered: Unleash Your Employees, Energize Your Customers, Transform Your Business* (Harvard Business Review Press, 2010), pp. 115–117.

34 Dylan Minor, Paul Brook, and Josh Bernoff, "Data from 3.5 Million Employees Shows How Innovation Really Works," *Harvard Business Review,* October 9, 2017.

35 "2020 Global State of Enterprise Analytics: Minding the Data-Driven Gap," MicroStrategy, https://www3.microstrategy.com/getmedia/db67a6c7-0bc5-41fa-82a9-bb14ec6868d6/2020-Global-State-of-Enterprise-Analytics.pdf.

36 Srividya Sridharan and Cinny Little, "Create the Culture Needed to Be Insights Driven," Forrester, June 7, 2022, https://www.forrester.com/report/create-the-culture-needed-to-be-insights-driven/RES177563 (accessible to Forrester clients).

37 "Digital Transformation Report 2023: CIO Priorities in a Dynamic Market," Randstad, https://randstad.us/digital-transformation-report-2023.

38 Melissa Agnes, "Information Silos Are Hurting Your Crisis Preparedness," Melissaagnes.com, April 12, 2016, https://melissaagnes.com/information-silos-are-hurting-your-crisis-preparedness/.

39 Leonard Kile, "New Business Rules Require Data Democratization,
    Forrester CX Speakers Urge," *Destination CRM,* June 9, 2022, https://
    www.destinationcrm.com/Articles/CRM-News/CRM-Featured-Articles/
    New-Business-Rules-Require-Data-Democratization-Forrester-CX-
    Speakers-Urge-153380.aspx.

40 Bill Gates, "The Age of AI Has Begun," *GatesNotes,* March 21, 2023,
    https://www.gatesnotes.com/The-Age-of-AI-Has-Begun.

41 Kenneth Chang, "Scientists Achieve Nuclear Fusion Breakthrough with
    Blast of 192 Lasers," *New York Times,* December 13, 2022, https://www.
    nytimes.com/2022/12/13/science/nuclear-fusion-energy-breakthrough.
    html.

42 Behnam Tabrizi, "How Microsoft Became Innovative Again,"
    Harvard Business Review, February 20, 2023, https://hbr.org/2023/02/
    how-microsoft-became-innovative-again.

43 PV Kannan with Josh Bernoff, *The Age of Intent: Using Artificial
    Intelligence to Deliver a Superior Customer Experience* (Amplify, 2019), pp.
    145–147.

INDEX

Oracle, 210
organizational change management. *See* change management
Outside In, 66

P

pandemic. *See* COVID-19
Parmer, Anne, 231
Pearsall, Matthew J., 173
people/process/technology, 22–23, 152–59
Philips, 14
Planview IdeaPlace, 178
PPP (Paycheck Protection Program), 7
predictive analytics, 71, 199
prioritizing outcomes, 16
product mindset, 119–22, 162

Q

Quaglio, Ken, 231
Qualtrics, 210

R

RadioShack, 224
Randstad, 142, 159, 208–9, 233, 235
    IT decision-maker survey, 208–9
    Workmonitor, 142
RASCI analysis, 81
responsive enterprise, 5, *See also* responsive enterprise transformation
    better financial performance of, 219–20
    future leaders of, 227–28
    maturity, 25–26, 217–21
    superior performance of, 25
    three dimensions of, 18–26
    transformation, 29–50
    will rule the future, 217–29
responsive enterprise transformation, 29–50
    embedding feedback loops, 37, 38, 46–48
    embracing systems thinking, 36, 38, 41–43
    empowered teams, 36–37, 38, 43–45
    exposing value, 36, 38, 39

four E's, 36–37
four-stage cycle, 35–48
    transformation matrix, 37–39
    who is responsible for, 36
RetailCo case study, 79–83, 135, 145
Ritz-Carlton, 59–60
root cause analysis, 146–48

S

Sadun, Raffaella, 84
Salesforce, 157, 207
Schadler, Ted, 177
Schantz, Rick, 113, 231
Schwab, Curt, 13, 233–35
Scott, JT, 133–36, 141, 231
scrum, 112
SEAL (change management steps), 87–89
Sears, 14, 224
service blueprinting, 147
service design, 70
shadow IT, 207
SharePoint, 182
silos, breaking down, 209–10
Simon, Herbert A., 72
Sims, Henry P., Jr, 173
Slack, 210
Southwest Airlines, 10
sprints, 112
    design sprints, 72–73
standup meetings, 112
Sun Also Rises, The, 226
supply-chain disruption, 12–13
Sweda, Rebecca, 87, 231
Switch, 86
systems thinking, 36, 38, 41–43, 75, 104, 125–26, 143–63
    elements of corporate systems, 152–59
    Five Whys, 148
    governance and performance frameworks, 158–59
    iceberg model, 149–52
    origins of, 149–52
    partners and ecosystems, 157–58
    people and organizations, 152–53

Printed in the USA
CPSIA information can be obtained
at www.ICGtesting.com
JSHW042030080624
64472JS00012B/57/J